현장 교실영어

원어민 영어 수업 따라하기

Actual Classroom Interactions

황기동 지음
Gregory Goguts 해설 및 감수

어문학사

머|리|말

　최근 선진국에서는 영어 교육의 흐름이 원어민이 아닌 자국인 중심으로 바뀌었다. 필자가 최근 영국 버밍엄대학교에서 TEFL을 학습할 때 영국인 교수들은 오랜 연구 결과 원어민이 아닌 자국인에 의한 영어 교육이 훨씬 효과적이라고 주장하였다. 실제 영어 자체의 이해, 언어 간의 기본적인 차이점에 대한 인식, 문화적인 차이 등을 고려할 때, 이런 주장은 상당한 설득력이 있다. 물론 여기에는 한국의 영어 선생님들이 영어로 영어를 가르치는 능력을 갖추어야 한다는 전제가 수반된다.

　영어권 나라에서 영어 교육을 받지 않고서도 교실에서 효과적으로 영어를 구사하여 교육을 하기 위해서는 다음 두 가지를 충족해야 한다고 생각한다. 첫째, 교실에서 사용하는 다양한 상용표현(formulaic expressions)을 숙지하고 활용할 수 있어야 한다. 원어민이 사용하는 상용 교실영어 표현을 충분히 익히고 있어야만 어색하지 않고 자연스런 영어를 구사할 수 있는 것이다. 둘째, 실제 외국인 수업을 참관하여 이들이 구사하는 영어 표현을 활용하고 수업 전개 방식을 연구하는 것이다. 즉 원어민의 교과 수업 진행 방식을 이해하기 위해서는 원어민 수업 과정을 수록한 다양한 자료를 이용하여 영어의 어휘, 문법, 말하기, 쓰기 등을 어떻게 자연스럽게 가르치는지를 이해해야 한다. 이를 위해 필자는 수년간 원어민 수업을 관리, 평가하면서 수시로 수집한 자료를 체계적으로 정리하였다. 이 책을 읽으면서 쉽고 간단한 영어 표현과 교과 진행 방식을 습득한다면 영어권 나라에 가지 않고도 충분히 영어로 영어를 가르칠 수 있다고 믿는다.

이 책은 원어민 선생님이 실제 영어 수업 과정에서 학생들과 대화한 내용을 가능한 원문 그대로 정리하였다. 원어민 선생님의 표현은 거의 전부 자연스러운 일상 교실영어 표현이지만, 학생들의 대답은 현장감을 살리기 위해 가능한 문법적인 오류를 수정하지 않았다. 그리고 각각의 대화문 다음에는 주요 표현에 대한 원어민 선생님의 해설을 첨부하였다. 원어민 선생님의 수업에 대한 원어민의 해설을 살펴보는 것도 많은 도움이 될 것으로 보인다. 그리고 각 주제의 서두에는 대화 내용의 원활한 이해를 위하여 필자가 간단히 우리말로 전체적인 내용을 해설하고, 때로 원어민 선생님의 교수 방법에 대해서도 간간이 언급하였다.

이 책은 원어민 선생님이 사용하는 교실영어 표현 및 수업 진행 방식과 다양한 영어 교수법에 대한 연구 자료로 활용될 수 있을 것이다. 본서가 영어 선생님 또는 영어로 수업을 해야 하는 선생님에게 현장 교실영어 수업을 실질적으로 이해하고 간접 경험하는 데에 많은 도움이 되기를 바란다.

2011년 7월

고출봉 아래에서 황 기 동

이|책|의|구|성

인사말을 나눈 후 복습과
관한 이야기로 시작한다.

T: Hello! How are you guys today?

Ss: We're doing good!

T: Excellent! Then I guess **we can ge**

Ss: Booyah!²⁾

T: Good! **Do you remember what**

Ss: No, we don't remember.

Okay. Let's review the last

ⓐ Native Teachers' Classroom Activities

본문에는 실제 원어민의 교실 수업 현장에서 있었던 대화를 수록하여 현장감을 높이고, 자신만의 효율적인 영어 수업을 만들어 볼 수 있도록 제시하였다. 또한 수업에서 주로 다룰 수 있는 주제를 총 8개로 분류하여 명확하게 내용을 파악하여 현장 수업에 대비할 수 있도록 하였다.

ⓑ Cartoon

본문의 내용과 연관을 가지면서 생활 속에서도 눈여겨 볼만한 그림 이야기를 넣어 학습할 때 지루하지 않도록 구성하였다.

rtoon] Plane Reservations

Reservations. May I help you?

Yes, I want to make reservations to Atlanta on June 2, on a flight after 5 o'clock if possible.

I can give yo on Flight 549 4:45 p.m., o leaving at 5:5

| 549 | ATLANTA |
| 864 | ATLANTA |

light 549 is due in at 7:51 p.m., 864 at

Do they serve dinner

ⓒ Main Topic
본문에서 다루고 있는 중심 주제를 간략하게 서술
하여 빠르게 내용을 파악하여 어떤 수업이 진행될
지 outline을 잡아 주었다.

Introduction

 선생님의 지시에 따라 교과 활동을 보조하는
하고, 학생들의 질문에 대답하고 있다.

T: And this is our T.A. I think he will i

Kiyoung: Hi, my name is Kiyoung, I

ess I've met some of y

...sing Words : 'to', 'too ,
confuse 'to', 'too', and 'two' : Two da
'too', 'two'를 혼동하지 마세요. 2월은 기다리기에

Expressions used

1) **We can get down to work** : We can begi
   수업 시작하겠습니다.

2) **Booyah!** : No real meaning, just an expre
   A fun motivating word. 부야! 구체적인 의미기
   미를 지닌다. 흥미 유발을 위한 감탄사.
   선생님이 학생들에게 교과 학습 활동을 시작
   oyah'라고 말하도록 지시하였음.

ⓓ Experssion used
실용적이고 유용한 구문에는 강조 표시를 하여
아래에 해설을 달아 놓았다. 특히 원어민이 직접
paraphrase 하여 실제 교실에서 어떤 대화가 오가
는지 알기 쉽도록 표현하였다.

이 | 책 | 의 | 목 | 차

Part 1 Greetings & Small Talk   인사말과 짧은 대화

Part 2 Vocabulary

Part 7 Game · · · · · · 게임

Part 8 Others · · · · · · 기타

Practice makes perfect.

연습함으로써 완벽해질 수 있다.

Part 1

Don't tell your friends about your indigestion;
"How are you!" is a greeting, not a question.
[Arthur Guiterman(1871~1943), American Writer]

당신의 친구에게 당신의 소화불량에 대해 이야기하지 마라.:
"How are you!"는 인사말이지 질문이 아니다.

Greetings & Small Talk
인사말과 짧은 대화

학습내용 ─────
학과 수업 시작 전 원어민 선생님과 학생들이 나눈 대화를 수록하였다. 학생들의 표현은 현장감을 살리고, 학습 자료로도 활용할 수 있도록 내용 수정 없이 그대로 수록하였다. 원어민 선생님의 유용한 표현에 대해서는 원어민이 직접 영어 해설을 첨부하였다. 또한 해설 다음에는 편의상 저자가 우리말로 해석 또는 보충 설명을 붙였다.

First Class

첫 시간

첫 수업 시간에 원어민 선생님이 우리말을 사용하지 말고, 영어로만 대화할 것을 지시하고 있다.

T=Teacher, S=Student, Ss=Students

T: Hi and welcome. I think you all know me. **Who was in my class before?** [1]

S: I was sir.

T: I remember you. Do you remember me?

S: Yes, sir.

T: So, do any of you have any questions? ⋯ No? OK. You should know that in my class there is no Korean; **Only English!** [2]

Ss: Yes, sir.

T: For most of you, you will have to know everything about conducting a briefing, whether it's formal or just informal.

Tip English

When the United States of America was formed, a vote was taken to decide what the official language of the US would be. English won, but only by one vote. Otherwise, the US would have been a German-speaking country. (미국이 형성될 때, 미국의 공식 언어를 무엇으로 할지 투표를 했습니다. 영어가 한 표 차로 이겼습니다. 그렇지 않았다면, 미국은 독일어를 말하는 국가가 되었을 것입니다.)

Expressions used

1) **Who was in my class before?** : Who was my student in a previous class? 지난 학기 내 수업을 들은 학생 있습니까?

2) **Only English!** : No speaking Korean! 영어만 사용하세요.

Greetings & Review
인사말과 복습

인사말을 나눈 후 복습을 하기 위한 대화이다. 자연스럽게 지난 시간에 관한 이야기로 시작한다.

T: Hello! How are you guys today?

Ss: We're doing good!

T: Excellent! Then I guess **we can get down to work.** [1]

Ss: **Booyah!** [2]

T: Good! **Do you remember what we learned last time?** [3]

Ss: No, we don't remember.

T: Okay. Let's review the last lesson.

Tip Confusing Words : 'to', 'too', and 'two'
Try not to confuse 'to', 'too', and 'two' : Two days is too long to wait. Do you think so too?
(어휘 'to', 'too', 'two'를 혼동하지 마세요.: 2일은 기다리기에 너무 길다. 너도 역시 그렇게 생각하니?)

Expressions used

1) **We can get down to work** : We can begin our work.
수업 시작하겠습니다.

2) **Booyah!** : No real meaning, just an expression similar to 'OK!'.
A fun motivating word. 부야! 구체적인 의미가 없으며, 'OK', 'Good'과 비슷한 의미를 지닌다. 흥미 유발을 위한 감탄사.
▶ 선생님이 학생들에게 교과 학습 활동을 시작할 때 불평하지 말고, 적극적으로 다 함께 'Booyah'라고 말하도록 지시하였음.

3) **Do you remember what we learned last time?** : Asking the students if they remember what was learned in the last class.
학생들에게 지난 시간에 학습한 것을 기억하는지 물을 때 사용하는 표현.

Good to See You!

 처음 만났을 때 사용하는 인사말에 대한 설명이다. 학생의 잘못된 응답을 수정하고 있다.

T: Good to see you again. Did you have a nice weekend?

S: Nice to see you.

T: 'Nice to see you' is wrong. You only say that the first time you meet someone. We've met a lot of times, haven't we?

S: Yes, we did.

T: So what should you say instead?

S: Nice to see you again.[1)]

T: Right.

Tip Synonyms of Nice

We had a nice supper. [delicious, tasty] (우리는 맛있는 저녁을 먹었다.)

The nice woman next door. [kind, friendly, likable] (옆집에 사는 친절한 여자)

We had a nice time on vacation. [enjoyable, pleasant, wonderful] (우리는 방학 때 즐거운 시간을 보냈다.)

What nice weather we are having. [good, fine, beautiful, lovely, mild] (오늘 날씨가 좋구나!)

Expressions used

1) **Nice to see you again**：Same as 'Good to see you again.'
다시 만나 반갑습니다.

Cartoon

[Cartoon] Checking out of a Hotel(퇴실)

선생님의 지시에 따라 교과 활동을 보조하는 어학 조교가 자신을 소개하고, 학생들의 질문에 대답하고 있다.

T: And this is our T.A. I think he will introduce himself.

Kiyoung: Hi, my name is Kiyoung, but you can call me K.

I guess I've met some of you before, but let me quickly introduce myself to you. I've been to the United States and Canada. And there I learned my English. I'm 22 and I go to Korea University.

I like reading books, watching movies, and listening to music. If you have any questions whatsoever, don't hesitate and come see me.

I will try to help you in whatever way I can. Or you may come by my office at any time. Thank you.

T: Do you have any questions for him?

S1: How many years have you been to the U.S.A. and Canada?

Kiyoung: I've been there for a total of 7 years.

Ss: Wow. Your English is good!

Kiyoung: Thank you.

S2: What is it like in Canada?[1)]

Kiyoung: Well⋯ Where I lived was very quiet and clean. There were even deer playing around the backyard.

S2: Wa! I want to go there too.

Introduction

Tip Canada

Canada is divided into ten provinces and two national territories ; The Yukon Territory and the Northwest Territories. However, the island of Greenland belongs to Denmark. (캐나다는 10개의 주와 2개의 국토로 나뉜다. : 유콘 영토와 북서 영토. 그러나 그린랜드는 덴마크에 속한다.)

Expressions used

1) **What is it like in Canada?** : What is Canada like? What is it like living in Canada? 캐나다는 살기가 어떻습니까?

수업 시작 전에 지난 주말의 활동에 대해 잡담을 나누면서, 학생들의 잘
못된 표현을 자연스럽게 수정하고 있다.

T: What did you do last weekend?

S1: I went to Seoul in Chunggae River. Chunggae River⋯ Um
very beautiful night seeing.

T: Night sight. **Was anything special happening?** [1]

S1: Ummm⋯

T: It was beautiful?

S1: Yes.

S2: Do you know Dream Hall? The theatre?

T: Yes.

S2: There is a speaker coming. [2]

T: How often do speakers come here?

S2: One time a year.

T: Not one time. Once.

S2: Once a year.

S3: Too many person.

T: People! One person. Two people.

S4: What do you like to do on your free time?

T: In your free time.

S4: In your free time.

S5: Would you like chocolate?

T: No, thank you.

S5: My mama said, "Don't eat a lot of chocolate", but I love chocolate!

S6: (when other students are chatting) Hey, be quiet.

T: Thank you. For this week, I want you to try and learn new adjectives when describing people.

Expressions used

1) **Was anything special happening?**: The teacher is asking the student if there was a special reason why (s)he went to Seoul.
선생님이 그 학생이 서울에 간 특별한 이유가 있는지 묻고 있다.

2) **There is a speaker coming**: The student is informing the teacher that there will be a guest speaker coming to the school.
학생이 학교에 초빙 인사가 온다는 것을 알리고 있다.

[Cartoon] Plane Reservations

열차를 놓쳐 피곤한 여행을 했던 학생의 이야기이다. 소란스러워지자 선생님이 각 그룹의 조장('captain'으로 지칭함)에게 영어로만 이야기할 것을 지시하고 있다.

T: Mr. Lim, you look awful today! **You look like you are wearing a Halloween mask!**[1] What happened?

Lim: How do you spell Halloween?

T: H.A.L.L.O.W.E.E.N.

Lim: Oh, well, I was traveling to Seoul last weekend and I was going to take the KTX.

T: Really? OK. Go on.

Lim: I was taking taxi to Pusan Station. But taxi driver drive too late.

T: The taxi driver drove too late?

Lim: Yes, so I missed the train.

T: How awful! So, what did you do?

Lim: I took Moogoonghwa train and arrived at Seoul at 2 a.m.

T: No wonder you look tired today.

Ss: (Students are talking to each other in Korean.)

T: No Korean speaking during my class, please!

Ss: OK. Sorry.

T: Captains, I want you to make sure everybody speak English and only English. OK?

Captains: OK.

Ss: Can we use the dictionary?

T: Yes, you may use dictionaries. But no Korean! Now, I want you to do exercise #1. **Take charge!**[2]

Captains: Take charge!

Tip Steam and Water

Steam fills 1,700 times as much space as the water that it has been boiled from. If you compress steam into a small container, it pushes against the sides. If there is a place or thing that the steam can move, such as a piston, the steam will force the piston outward. When the steam cools, it turns back into water, takes less space, and the piston returns to its original position. Early steam engines used the principle to pump water out of mines. (증기는 끓으면 물보다 1,700배의 면적을 채운다. 스팀을 작은 용기 속에 밀어 넣으면, 그것은 양 옆으로 밀고 나간다. 피스톤과 같은 스팀이 이동시킬 수 있는 물체가 있으면, 증기는 피스톤을 밖으로 밀어낸다. 증기가 식으면 물이 되고, 부피가 적어지며 피스톤은 원래의 위치로 돌아온다. 초기의 증기 엔진은 이 원리를 이용하여 광산에서 물을 펌프로 빼내었다.)

Expressions used

1) **You look like you are wearing a Halloween mask!** : Your face is tired and sad looking. 너의 얼굴이 매우 피곤하고 슬퍼 보인다.

2) **Take charge!** : A motivating expression meaning the students should take command of their learning. It implies encouragement that you can do it : 'Go for it' or 'Take (the) initiative'. 학생이 자신들의 학습에 주도권을 쥐어야 한다는 것을 의미하는 표현이다. 그것은 '당신도 할 수 있다'는 격려의 의미로, 'Go for it' 또는 'Take (the) initiative'와 유사한 의미를 지닌다.

Blind Date

미팅

 지난주에 한 미팅 이야기이다. 아래에 등장하는 미국식 이름 – Tyson, Victor, Charlie 등 – 은 원어민 선생님이 학생들을 부르기 쉽게 붙인 별명이다.

Dialogue A

미팅하는 파트너의 외적 조건에 대한 이야기이다.

....

T: Who had a blind date last weekend? (3 students raise hands.) Tyson, Victor and Charlie?

S1: Except Charlie. (One more student raises his hand.)

T: And David, too? Where were the girls from?

S1: English majors from K. University.

T: Did you match the couples?

S1: Yes, matched random.

T: Not random, randomly.

S1: But Tyson chose his girl.

T: So you chose the prettiest one?

S2: No, he chose the richest one. (Students all laugh, "Hahaha!")

T: But how did you know that she was the richest?

Tyson: I looked on the Internet. (Tyson tells the story.)

T: So did you get her phone number?

Tyson: She called me.

T: So Tyson, she is interested in you but you are not interested in her?

Tyson: Me? No, I'm interested!

Blind Date

T: Yes?

Tyson: Yes, I'm interested.

S2: Tyson is interested in every woman!

Victor: My girl was not good but character was very good.

S4: He had two partners. Do you know "Sleepy" Choi? **She made a chance to me a blind date.**[1]

T: So, Victor, the girl was not pretty but had a good personality. So, will you see her again?

Victor: Um···, not··· not···, hmm··· No!

T: Let's take out the personality adjectives. Because she is not pretty, even though she has a nice personality, you will never meet her. **If your thinking is very deep thinking, it's very strong.**[2]

Though, so, Victor, **you might have shallow thinking.**[3]

(Students all laugh, "Hahaha!")

Victor: Maybe I'll meet her. (Haha)

T: I was just joking.

Victor: Me too.

T: How was the second girl?

Victor: Good.

T: 'Good' means pretty?

Victor: Pretty and good personality.

S2: A lot of students think a lot about the appearance.

S1: Yeah.

T: Yes?

S1: Yes.

Expressions used

1) **She made a chance to me a blind date.**
   문법에 맞게 수정하면 다음과 같다.
   그녀는 나에게 미팅을 주선했다.
   ● She set up [arranged] a blind date for me.
   ● She set me up on a blind date.
   ● She asked me out on a blind date.

2) **If your thinking is very deep thinking, it's very strong** : This is foreigner talk. We should say "If your thought comes from within, that's a very strong opinion". 이것은 외국인이 이야기했다. 우리는 "만일 네 생각이 내면에서 우러나왔다면 그건 매우 굳건한 판단이다."라고 말한다.

3) **you might have shallow thinking** : This is also foreigner talk. We should say "You may think superficially". 이것도 외국인이 이야기했다. 우리는 "너는 피상적으로 생각한다."라고 말한다.

Dialogue B :

사귀고 있는 간호학교 여학생에 대한 이야기이다.

....

T: When you have blind dates what happens?

Blind Date 미팅

Ss: When they like each other.

S1: Actually, I don't like blind dates. I like natural meeting. I don't think I can't understand someone in a very short period, so I would like to meet someone in church or school or places like that.

T: Who has a girlfriend right now?

S2: Me.

T: Do you meet very often, or just call many times?

S2: We call many times.

S3: Because many people see that couple, they feel uncomfortable and have hard time to meet.

T: So they are a very famous couple!

Ss: Yes.

T: So, Charles, you haven't said anything today. You have been very quiet.

Charles: Um··· When I was freshman, I had a pen pal in nursing school. But I didn't like writing letters. I was tired of writing, so our connection was cut. But when I was in third grade, the nursing school came to our school.

T: So you saw the same woman, or different?

Charles: Nursing school came in groups, so she was included in the group.

T: She is coming? Or she already came?

Charles: She already came.

T: So you met her.

Charles: Yes, she was a pretty girl.

Ss: Oh.

Charles: So we went to Star Bakery, and we had ice cream.

Ss: 팥빙수.

Charles: Yes, 팥빙수. Because we went to close sea training I had to go there, so our meeting was not good.

T: You like this girl?

Charles: I was interested in meeting girlfriends.

T: Well, good luck.

Charles: Thank you.

T: And David, you are very quiet back there.

David: I like a very pretty woman.

T: A specific pretty woman or any pretty woman?

David: One pretty woman.

T: Is she a university student?

David: She goes to K. University.

T: Is she a high school friend?

David: She is my church friend.

T: Does she know you like her?

Blind Date

David: I don't know.

T: Did you tell her that you like her?

David: No.

T: Why?

Charley: He is very shy.

David: Shy, shy. She is the only woman I liked.

T: OK. Cy, you're back there, very quiet also.

Duke: He likes cyber chatting.

T: So do you like chatting to Americans also?

Duke: No, just Koreans.

T: Have you ever met the women you chat with?

Duke: No.

Ss: Yes! A lot of women.

T: No!

Charley: He's lying.

T: So you meet only women?

Charley: Only women.

T: How do you meet only women?

Charley: The chat room name is Military Love. (Students all laugh, "Hahaha!")

T: So you go to this café and all the women are there.

Charley: **I'm very sorry but I don't really want to talk about**

that.[1]

T: That's OK. That was a very good and polite way to say that you don't like the topic.

Jess: It's none of your business.[2]

T: No, that is very impolite.

Jess: I'm very good at speaking impolitely. (Students all laugh, "Hahaha!")

T: So, "I'm sorry; I'm not comfortable[3]; I don't want to talk about this", is a very good way to say that you don't want to talk about something.

Expressions used

1) **I'm very sorry but I don't really want to talk about that**: The student does not want to talk about that topic.
학생은 그 문제에 대해 이야기하고 싶어하지 않는다.

2) **It's none of your business**: A common expression that means your question is personal and I will not answer it.
질문이 개인적이어서 대답하지 않을 것이다는 표현.

3) **I'm not comfortable**: Talking about the topic makes the speaker uncomfortable. 그 문제에 대해 이야기하기가 불편하다.

Movies

최근에 본 영화에 대한 대화이다. 선생님이 형용사(saddening)의 의미를
확인하고, 영화 선정이 정서에 맞지 않았다고 지적하고 있다.

T: What movie did you see recently?

S: The movie 'If Only' is very romantic and **saddening.**[1]

T: You mean melancholy?

S: Yes, a little. I watched it when I was single.

T: When you didn't have a girlfriend?

S: Yes, after I broke up with my girlfriend.

T: Hmm. You should have seen a comedy or something to cheer you up! **'If Only' probably brought you down.**[2]

S: Hhhhh.

 Tip Admission vs Admittance

'Admission' usually refers to a permission to enter a public place, or the price of a ticket for entry.
'Admittance' is a more formal word for the act of entering a private place not usually open to
the public. (Admission[입장, 입장료]은 대개 공공장소에 들어가는 것을 허가하거나, 입장권의 가격을 의미한다.
Admittance[입장 허가]는 공공에게 개방되지 않은 사적인 곳에 들어가는 행위를 나타내는 공식적인 단어이다.)

Expressions used

1) **saddening :** The student used this as an adjective to mean 'to
make someone sad.' I would say 'sad' rather than 'saddening'.
학생은 슬프다는 의미로 'saddening'이라고 했지만 'saddening'보다는 'sad'가 더 좋다.
e.g. It's saddening that the students don't study hard in class.
학생들이 수업 중 공부를 하지 않는 것은 나를 슬프게 한다.

2) **'If Only'** probably brought you down : 'If Only' is the title of a sad
movie. 'Brought you down' means 'made you sad'.
'If Only'는 슬픈 영화의 제목이다. 'Brought you down'은 '낙담하게 하다'는 의미이다.

Watching Opera

 지난주 감상한 오페라에 대한 대화이다. 오페라에 대한 이야기를 하면서 학생들이 자신들의 표현 능력이 부족함을 아쉬워하고 있다.

T: Julis, what happened on Wednesday?

Julis: Came opera on Wednesday.

T: **There was an opera?** [1)](#)

Julis: Yes, there was an opera.

T: **Was it anybody's first time to see an opera?** [2)](#)

(One student raises hand.)

T: What was your first impression of the opera?

S1: It was very boring.

T: Really? I've never seen an opera, but I've heard that they are very powerful and interesting.

S1: I think they were low level. **It was very amateur and had also a bad environment.** [3)](#)

T: You said that you have seen an opera before. How was this opera compared to the other opera that you have seen?

S1: It was very⋯아 단어가 딸리네⋯ It was the worst opera on Wednesday. I was⋯ I came to Pusan⋯ I watched Carmen.

T: Yes, you guys saw Carmen last year.

S2: That was a very good version, I mean, yes.

T: What was the name of the opera on Wednesday?

S2: Love Medicine.

S3: Medicine of Love.

S1: Love Potion.

T: Was it originally Korean?

S1: I think it was from France or Italy. We thought it was very bad compared to Carmen or other operas.

T: When you saw Carmen, was it in Korean or English?

S1: They were translated in Korean, so we could understand.

T: Did anybody enjoy the opera on Wednesday?

S3: It was so terrible!

S2: In the orchestra, there was some woman. She was my violin teacher, so I'm so embarrassed.

T: But it's wonderful that she was there!

S2: But the opera was so bad.

T: That's too bad.

Watching Opera

오페라 감상

 Soap Opera

The term Soap Opera came about when they were first broadcast on radio during the 1930s. Their main sponsers were soap manufacturers. ('연속극'이라는 용어는 1930년대 라디오로 처음 방송되었을 때 나타난 것으로, 그것들의 주 후원자는 비누 제조업자였다.)

Expressions used

1) **There was an opera?**: The speaker is 'asking' this as a way of showing the student interest in the topic. This rhetorical question indicates wanting more information.
선생님은 학생에게 그 화제가 재미있다는 것을 보여주기 위해서 질문을 하고 있다. 이런 수사적 질문은 더 많은 정보를 원한다는 것을 나타낸다.

2) **Was it anybody's first time to see an opera?**: The speaker is asking if this is the first time anyone has been to or seen an opera. 선생님은 이번에 본 오페라가 처음인 사람이 있는지 묻고 있다.

3) **It was very amateur and had also a bad environment**: Not done at a professional level. The bad environment is probably the student's attempt at saying that the stage, scenery, etc. didn't look very good. 전문가 수준이 아니었다. 나쁜 환경이란 말은 아마 학생이 무대와 장면 등이 좋지 않았다는 것을 말하려고 한 것이다.

[Cartoon] Making a Date

Game

지난주에 한 격구에 대한 대화이다. 격구에 대한 이야기 도중 학생의 과거시제 사용을 자연스럽게 수정하고 있다.

T: Tell me what you guys did during the week or anything special you've done?

S1: (Raises his hand.)

T: Yes, Mr. Kim.

S1: The juniors played '격구' yesterday.

T: Ah. That's why some guys are wounded.

'격구' **is the game 50 on 50.**[1] Right? 5 balls and 2 keepers.

S1: Yep.

T: So, did you win the game?

S1: Of course, we win!

T: You guys win?

S1: Yes.

T: **Didn't you say 'yesterday?'**[2] Then you should say 'won'.

S1: We won!

Expressions used

1) **'격구' is the game 50 on 50**: Two teams, 50 people on each team. '50 people vs 50 people.'
   두 팀으로, 각 팀이 50명이다. '50명 대 50명.'

2) **Didn't you say 'yesterday?'**: The student made a past tense verb mistake and the teacher is correcting the student's faulty grammar. 학생은 과거시제를 잘못 사용하였으며, 선생님은 학생의 잘못된 문법을 고치고 있다.

Baseball Game

 지난주 세계 야구 선수권(WBC)에 대한 이야기이다. 대화 도중 전치사 'in'의 용법을 수정하고, 'same thing'의 의미를 확인하고 있다.

T: Now which teams are left; who will go to the finals?

Ss: Cuba[kuba] and Japan.

T: Not [kuba].

S4: Cuba[kjuːbə].

T: Yes, Cuba. **Now that you have lost, do you care about the game?**[1]

S5: I hope Cuba wins.

T: Why?

S5: I hate the Japan.

T: You hate Japan. Do you hate just the team, or the country Japan?

S5: Country.

S1: We thought that what Ichiro said was rude.

S2: He said to news, "I will show you that Korea and Taiwan will never win Japan, never beat Japan in 30 years later."

T: In 30 years, not 'in 30 years later'.

S2: In 30 years. OK. So I don't like Ichiro either.

T: Okay. I understand. In the major league he is the best hitter. In Cuba, who is the best hitter?

S5: I don't know. I don't care. Just Japan. Just concerned about Japanese team.

T: When is the game?

S3: Monday. American Monday.

S4: Nina, how popular is Ichiro in US?

T: He is very popular. Okay, besides the baseball game⋯ Sorry Britney, you were not very interested in this subject.

S4: Haha.

S7: It's Okay.

T: What did you do over the weekend? (raising her hand) Did everyone go home?

Ss: (Students who went home raise their hands.)

S3: No, I stayed here.

T: Benjamin, you stayed here?

S3: Yes.

T: Why?

S3: I was doing your homework.

Ss: Hahaha⋯

T: Good student. How about you? (Looks at student 1.)

S1: I didn't check the list of liberty, so I can't go home.

T: So when you want to go on liberty, you have to sign something?

S1: Yes.

T: So the rest of you went home?

Ss: Yes.

Baseball Game

T: Did you do anything special this weekend?

S4: Same thing.

T: **What is the same thing?** [2]

S4: I stayed with my friends⋯ Uh⋯ All night. We watch TV and drink some beverage and we talk about life⋯

T: You mean your college friends or high school friends?

S4: No, no, my older friends, and high school friends, and outside friends.

Tip Origin of 'Tennis'

'Tennis' comes from a French word, 'tenez' meaning 'hold' or 'take' 'which a player called out to his opponent to attract their attention. (테니스는 '잡다', '가지다'를 의미하는 프랑스 어, 'tenez'에서 유래된 것이다. 주의를 끌기 위해서 선수는 상대편에게 'tenez'라고 소리치는 것이다.)

Expressions used

1) **Now that you have lost, do you care about the game?** : The teacher is asking the students if they care about the results of the World Baseball Classic between Japan and Cuba now that Korea has been eliminated. 한국이 배제된 이상 일본과 쿠바와의 세계 야구 시합 결과에 학생들이 관심이 있는지를 묻고 있다.

2) **What is the same thing?** : The student said that he or she did the 'same thing' when he/she went home for the weekend, but the teacher does not understand what the student means by 'same thing.' 'Same thing as what?' 학생은 주말에 집에 갔을 때 '같은 것'을 했다고 말했지만, 선생님은 학생의 말 'same thing'의 의미를 모른다. "어떤 같은 일 말이지?"

Current Issues

 지난밤 시합과 시사 문제에 대한 가벼운 잡담이다. 선생님이 한일 관계에 대한 이야기를 'bad blood'(뿌리 깊은 미움)로 요약하고 있다.

T: How did the game go last night?

Terry: It was good.[1]

T: Is that the only thing? What else is going on in this country?

Noa: President went to America yesterday.

T: Why did he visit America? What was the purpose?

Chris: To talk about North Korea problem.

T: So did they find some solution or answer?

Key: Actually the news is no solution. It's just talk.

T: What was his reason for going to Japan? Is it the same reason?

Chris: No, the relation with South Korea.

T: Was it a successful mission?

Ss: No.

T: Korea and Japan don't agree about their history.

Bearwolf: Yatsguni.

T: Did they discuss the Dokdo problem? Elly, was anything accomplished; did they finish with any agreement?

Elly: It's impossible to agree with Japan.

T: **We say that they have bad blood.**[2]

Current Issues

Tip American President
The youngest ever president of the United States was the 26th president, Theodore Roosebelt(1858~1919), who was 42 when he entered office; he was President from 1901 to 1909. (미국의 가장 젊은 대통령은 26대 데오도르 루즈벨트였다. 그가 집무를 시작했을 때 42세였으며, 1901년부터 1909년까지 대통령이었다.)

Expressions used

1) **It was good** : The game was good or interesting.
시합이 좋고 재미있었다.

2) **We say that they have bad blood** : 'Bad blood' means that two people or two countries have a bad history together and, therefore, don't get along well. Here, it is a reference to many Korean's feelings toward Japan.
'나쁜 피'는 두 사람 또는 두 나라가 좋지 못한 역사를 공유하고 있어서, 잘 지내지 못한다는 것을 의미한다. 여기에서는 일본에 대한 많은 한국인들의 감정을 언급하고 있다.

Driver License

운전 면허증

 주말 운전 면허 시험에 실패한 학생에게, 오히려 더 뛰어난 운전자가 될 수 있다고 격려하고 있다.

T: Hi, everyone! How was your weekend?

Ss: Good. Bad…

T: Bad? I'm sorry to hear that. What happened?

S: Driver license.

T: You got a driver license? That's great.

S: Um… I failed.

T: Oh! That's too bad!

S: I failed three times. [1]

T: Well, at least you are getting to be a better driver.

S: Yes.

T: In my opinion Korean drivers are dangerous.

Ss: ….

Terry: How about you? Mr. Kim ?

S2: My girlfriend and I went to Japan.

T: Wow! Did you have fun?

S2: It was very nice and I had fun.

Expressions used

1) **I failed three times :** I didn't pass the driving test three times.
운전 면허 시험에 3번이나 통과하지 못했다.

What's Up?

길에서 우연히 만났을 때의 인사말 중에서 'What's Up?' 의미와 응답
방법에 대해 설명하고 있다.

T: Hi, everyone. What do you guys usually say when you see
a friend on a street?

Ss: We say, "Hello" or "How are you?".

T: Have you guys heard people saying "What's up?"

Ss: Yeah, many times. But we don't exactly know what that
means.

T: "What's up" asks if there is anything special in your life
or simply what's happening. As people use it so much,
it has become a common greeting expression. But know
that even if "what's up" is a question, you are not always
expecting an answer when you say it. Also keep in mind
that it's an informal expression, so use it in a right time at a
right place.

Tip Synonyms of Say

I heard her say that she has read the book. [remark, comment, mention] (그녀가 그 책을 읽었다고
언급하는 것을 들었다.)
How do you say 'cloth'? [pronounce] ('천'을 어떻게 발음하니?)
She said that I would have to work much harder. [explained, announced] (내가 좀 더 열심히 일해
야 할 거라고 그녀가 설명했다.)

Expressions used

1) **Know that**: 'You should know/remember that'의 명령문

Talking behind One's Back

험담하다

 관용어의 의미를 실례를 들어 구체적으로 설명하고 있다. 그리고 나서 선생님을 비방하지 말라고 훈시하고 있다.

T: Do you guys say bad things about a friend when he or she is not present?

Ss: Not really….

T: Oh, come on. I know you guys have so much fun talking behind someone's back.

Ss: What? What does that mean?

T: Talking behind someone's back? Think about it. If you want to do something your friend doesn't like, wouldn't you want your friend not to know about it? It's the same thing. When you talk behind someone, you are talking about something he wouldn't want to hear. Try not to do this or do not get caught when you do! Especially, never ever talk behind my back! Or I'll fail you.

Tip Usage of 'Not'
Where you put 'not' can change the meaning of a sentence. 'He is trying not to win' is different from 'He is not trying to win'. ('Not'을 두는 위치가 문장의 의미을 바꾼다. '그는 이기지 않으려고 애쓴다'와 '그는 이기려고 애쓰지 않는다'는 다르다.)

Expressions used

1) **Come on:**The expression is used to show that the students didn't tell truth. 상대방의 말이 진실이 아닐 때 사실을 촉구하는 의미로 쓰이는 관용 어구이다.

Call It a Day

선생님이 수업을 끝마칠 때 쓰는 관용 표현의 의미에 대해 학생이 질문
하자 선생님이 동의어를 사용하여 설명하고 있다.

T: Okay now, let's go to the next chapter! Go to the page
168, class!

S: Awwwwww···

T: Oh, come on. Stop whining.

Ss: But professor, we only have two minutes before the bell
rings.

T: Um··· Okay. Since you guys were such good boys during
the class, I'm going to call it a day.

Ss: Eh? What do you mean by "call it a day"?

T: You don't know what "call it a day" is? What have I taught
you guys? It means that class is dismissed.

Ss: Awesome!

Tip Words with '-ph'
Words that include 'ph' (pronounced 'f') as part of the spelling come from the Greek, as in
'graphic' and 'photograph'. (철자의 일부로 'Ph'('프'로 발음됨)를 포함하는 단어들은 '그래픽'과 '사진'처럼
그리스 어에서 유래된 것이다.)

Expressions used

1) **Come on** : Let's get started. Let's get going.
'자! 시작하자'는 의미를 가진 구어적인 표현이다.

Part 2

Words are like leaves; and where they most abound,
much fruit of sense is rarely found.
[Alexander Pope From(1688~1744), English Poet]

말은 나뭇잎과 같다. : 가장 무성할 때에는
의미 있는 열매가 거의 없다.

Vocabulary
어휘

학습내용 ─────────
여기에서는 원어민의 어휘에 연
관된 수업 내용을 정리하였다.
원어민은 우리나라 말을 사용하
지 않으므로 가장 쉬운 방법으
로 어휘의 의미를 설명하려고 노
력하였다. 내용은 먼저 일반적인
단어, 복합어, 단어 간의 비교,
어휘 연습 및 복습의 순서로 정
리하였다.

Muggy

수업을 시작하기 전에 더운 날씨를 나타내는 형용사 'humid'에 대해 설명하고 있다. 그리고 반의어인 'Freeze'도 간접적으로 설명하고 있다.

T: How are you today?

S: Tired. How about you?

T: I'm OK. It's very hot today. But the air-conditioning is not working. How is the weather today? What do you call this kind of weather?

S: Humid.

T: Humid, or another word?

S: Wet.

T: Muggy. It's really sticky and muggy··· **My supervisor will come to our class in a moment.**[1]

S: Oh, no. We doesn't want.

T: Why does it make you nervous? **Do you freeze?**[2] You don't have to salute to him.

Expressions used

1) **My supervisor will come to our class in a moment**:The teacher's supervisor will be coming to observe the class.
수업 감독관이 수업을 관찰하기 위해 올 것이다.

2) **Do you freeze?**:The teacher is asking if the student gets so nervous when speaking or visiting with a high-ranking officer that (s)he can't speak. 학생이 고위 장교와 말하거나 대화를 나눌 때 너무 긴장해서 말을 할 수 없는지를 묻고 있다.

[Cartoon] Summer

Summit

휴가 중 고향에서 산행하러 갔던 이야기를 하면서 산 정상을 영어로 어떻게 표현하는가를 설명하고 있다.

S: My hometown is Daejon, so I have to spend so long time to my home.

T: **Not so long.**[1]

S: It's long.

T: Three hours?

S: Three hours. We went out 5 o'clock, so I arrived my home 9 o'clock, 10 o'clock. I slept on Saturday. On Sunday I went to hiking on a mountain in Daejon. On mountain, I can see all sides of Daejon.

T: How long did it take from the bottom of the mountain to the top?

S: About three hours.

T: What do we call the top of the mountain?

S: Hmm··· the top?

T: Okay, the top. What do we call the top of the mountain? We have two words.

S: Ah, summit.

T: OK, summit, that's one, and the other one is peak. We call it the peak of the mountain. You said that at the peak of the mountain, you could see all of Daejon, but is it pretty, the city?

S: Hmm, no, pretty, but meaningful.

Summit

산 정상

Tip It's vs Its

Be careful when you are writing 'it's' (a contraction of either 'it is' or 'it has') and 'its' (which means 'a characteristic of or something that belongs to it), e.g. It's a nice day for a picnic. A sparrow built its nest in a tree in our back yard. ('it is' 또는 'it has'의 축약형인 'it's'와, 성질이 있는 또는 그것에 속하는 것을 의미하는 'its'를 유의하세요. 예. 오늘은 소풍 가기 좋은 날이다. 참새 한 마리가 우리 뒤뜰의 나무에 자신의 둥지를 틀었다.)

Expressions used

1) **Not so long**: It doesn't take much time going to Daejon.
   (대전에 가 본 원어민 선생님은 대전까지 멀지 않다고 말하고 있다.)

Blog

블로그

 홈페이지의 이용에 대해 이야기하면서 블로그의 어원에 관한 설명을 하고 있다.

T: How many of you use the Internet?

Ss: Me! I use Internet everyday! (Most of the students raise their hands.)

T: Then I guess most of you are familiar with personal home pages. For example, Cyworld Mini Homes are called 'blogs'.

Ss: Yes, we know what they are.

T: Who can tell me why people make them and how they are used?

S1: I think people make home pages because of communication. Young people want to communicate online and homepage is great for that.

S2: We can also make new friends. People can see other people website and learn, and be closer.

T: Do any of you know what BLOG stands for?

S3: I think it is black plus egg. It like a mystery and no one knows before visiting.

T: BLOG is a combined word. WEB plus LOG! (Writes it on the board.)

It is a log you post on the Web, on the Internet.[1]

Blog

블로그

Tip Computer terms

Many computer terms are new uses for old words like 'boot' (to start up a computer), 'mouse' (the device that is used to work on screen), and 'bookmark' (to record an Internet address on your computer).

(많은 컴퓨터 용어 '부트'(켜다), '마우스(스크린을 움직이기 위해 사용되는 장치), '북마크(컴퓨터에 인터넷 주소를 기록해 두는 것)' 는 있던 단어를 새롭게 사용한 것이다.)

Expressions used

1) **It is a log you post on the Web, on the Internet**: a BLOG is a personal log that you post (display) on the Internet.

   블로거는 여러분이 인터넷에 게시하는 개인적인 기록이다.

Innovations

 먼저 선생님이 혁신 제품의 의미와 그 영향에 대해 토론할 것을 토의 과제로 제시하고 있다.

Question : 토론에 앞서 학생들에게 'innovations'의 의미가 무엇인지 설명해 주기를 요청하고 있다.

Consider all of the modern innovations that you have just discussed. In general, do you think the world is better or worse because of them? Explain.

....

T: Innovations. What does that mean?

S1: Improve…

T: Yes. You can improve the world. Think about new innovations. Can you give examples?

Ss: Fax machines, cell phones, beepers, microwaves, etc.

T: **Will the world be better or worse** (with the innovations)?[1]

Ss: Good.

T: Why did the world become better with the microwave oven?

Ss: (They are shouting several answers.)

T: All these also have bad things. What are they?

S: Pollution.

T: Right. The world became polluted. Why do those things pollute the world?

Ss: Garbage, soil, dirty water…

T: Yes, innovations sometimes cause problems. They have some things negative and some things positive. Then, what should we do about these problems?

Ss: ….

Tip System of measurements

The ancient Egyptians had a system of measurements that was based on the human body. The smallest unit, based on the hand, was a digit (which means (the breath of) a finger). Four digits made a palm. The distance between the little finger and thumb of an outstretched hand was called a span. A cubit was equal to 2 spans, 7 palms, or the distance from fingertips to elbow. (고대 이집트인은 인간의 신체에 기초를 둔 측량 단위를 가지고 있었다. 손에 기초를 둔 가장 작은 단위는 손가락(의 넓이)를 의미하는 디지트였다. 4디지트는 한 손바닥이었다. 뻠은 손의 새끼손가락과 엄지손가락 사이의 거리는 한 뼘이었다. 큐빗은 2뼘, 7손바닥, 또는 손가락 끝에서 팔꿈치까지의 거리였다.)

Expressions used

1) **Will the world be better or worse** (with the innovations)**?** : Has life become easier or more difficult? The speaker is asking the students if the world has become a better place or a worse place by using these innovations.
삶이 더 쉬워질 것인가, 더 어려워질 것인가? 선생님은 이런 혁신 제품을 사용함으로써 세상이 더 좋아질 것인지, 나빠질 것인지를 묻고 있다.

Hands Free

핸즈프리

 먼저 토론에서는 '해결책'을 제시하는 것이 중요하다고 강조한 뒤에, 운전 중에 사용하는 무선 통신 기기의 용도에 대해 설명할 것을 지시하고 있다.

T: When you talk about something bad or the disadvantages of, for example, cellular phones, cloning, you must give a solution. You must offer a solution. For example, if you're talking on the phone while driving, you can cause an accident and it is very dangerous. **The government says we shouldn't answer the phone while driving,**[1] but everybody talks on the phone while driving. So, we made or invented something. What is it? So, what do we use when we drive?

S: Hands free.

T: O.K. You use hands free. **Why is hands free good?** [2]

S: You can drive and talk.

T: Good.

Expressions used

1) **Government says we shouldn't answer the phone while driving**：The student is referring to the government's warning that driving and talking on the phone is something one shouldn't do because it is dangerous. 학생은 전화하면서 운전하거나 말하는 것은 위험하기 때문에 하지 않아야 하는 것이라는 정부의 경고를 언급하고 있다.

2) **Why is hands free good?**：Why is having a hands free cell phone in your car (one that you don't need to open or push buttons to answer) a good thing? 차 안의 무선 기기(응답하기 위해 버튼을 열거나 누를 필요가 없는 휴대전화)를 소지하는 것은 왜 좋은가?

Double Standard

 남자들의 이중적인 사고에 대한 대화이다. 어휘 해체(lexical decomposition) 방식을 이용하여 쉽게 설명하고 있다.

T: OK, let me ask you something. Do you guys know what 'double standard' means?

Ss: Umm….

T: Well, it's two words, 'double' and 'standard'. What's 'double' mean?

Ss: Umm, two?

T: Yeah! And what about 'standard'? (pause) It's a rule. So, 'double standard' means two rules. Now let's think about this. **Don't many men go and do 'bang-bang?'** [1]

Ss: (laughing)

T: But still, like you guys said, most men want their wives to be a virgin when they marry. But, if all men go 'bang', who can men marry? It's contradictory. A man wants his mate to be a virgin, while he also wants to have fun with other women. This is a double standard.

Expressions used

1) **Don't many men go and do 'bang-bang?'** : The teacher is using a euphemism to speak on the topic of having sex. 'Don't a lot of man have one-night stands[have sex for one night]?'
선생님은 성관계에 대하여 언급하기 위해 완곡어법을 사용하고 있다. '많은 남자들이 하룻밤 관계를 맺지 않느냐?'

방학을 마친 뒤 첫 시간에 방학 전 학습했던 항생제의 개념을 복습하고 있다.

T: Did you have a good vacation?

Ss: Yes!

T: How was your vacation? Mine was really great. I spent a lot of time with my family, and it was a very meaningful time for me. Since we all had a good time, I think that now we should concentrate on studying again. **Alright?** [1]

Ss: Okay! We are ready.

T: To warm up, let's see if you still remember what we learned before the long 3 week vacation. Who can tell me what an antibiotic is? We studied it a month ago.

S1: Antibiotic is something against bio. It means someone is not in good health.

T: Um··· Not quite! You must have forgotten everything during the vacation. Who else would like to try?

S2: **Antibiotic is a substance you take to fight virus or bacteria.** [2]

For example, you take antibiotic when you have disease. When you are sick, you take antibiotics to cure your body.

T: **Who can give me an example?** [3]

S3: It is like penicillin or Tylenol.

Antibiotic

T: Well, Tylenol is not an antibiotic. It is the name of a drug. It is a pill you take when you have a headache. We should concentrate on studying again.

Tip Effect vs Affect

The noun 'effect' goes with the verb 'affect'. It had no effect on me; it didn't affect me. The verb 'effect' has a different meaning, to make happen. (명사 'effect'는 동사로는 'affect'를 사용한다. 동사 'effect'는 '초래하다', '성취하다'는 의미를 가진다.)

Expressions used

1) **Alright?** : Are you O.K.? Do you agree with me? 준비되었습니까?

2) **Antibiotic is a substance you take to fight virus or bacteria** : 관사가 탈락된 문장으로 문법에 맞게 수정하면 다음과 같다.
   ▶ An antibiotic is a substance you take to fight[fight off, fight against] a virus or a bacteria. 항생제는 바이러스나 박테리아를 퇴치하는 물질입니다.

3) **Who can give me an example?** : Who can name some antibiotics? Give an example of an antibiotic.
   항생제의 명칭을 말해 볼 사람은? 항생제의 예를 들어 보세요.

Article

관사

중의적인 의미를 지닌 'article'의 개념에 대해 구체적인 예를 들어 설명하고 있다.

T: Many Korean students have a lot of problems with articles. So, what is an article?

S1: Newspaper?

T: No! We are talking about writing.

S2: We can't even make a guess! [1]

T: Alright then. Articles are the words 'a, an, the'.

Ss: Ah.

T: You don't say "He went to United states" but instead "He went to the United States."

Tip Usage of 'An'

'An' is the indefinite article used before words beginning with a vowel, as in 'an apple', and before words beginning with a vowel sound, as in 'an hour'. ('An'은 'an apple'과 같이 모음으로 시작하는 단어 앞이나, in 'an hour'와 같이 모음으로 시작하는 단어 앞에 사용되는 부정관사이다.)

 Expressions used

1) **We can't even make a guess!** : The student is telling the teacher that they don't know the answer, so they won't even try to guess at the correct answer.
답을 몰라 정답을 추측조차 할 수 없다고 학생들이 선생님에게 말하고 있다.

Synonym

 첫 시간에 원어민 선생님이 조교를 소개한 뒤에 'synonym'의 의미를 묻고 있다. 마지막에 학생이 생략어구(fragment—About the liberty)로 말하자 생략되지 않은 완전한 문장으로 말할 것을 지시하고 있다. 일반적으로 생략어구는 겸손하지 못한 표현으로 간주한다.

T: Hello, everybody.

Ss: Hello.

T: My name is John and I am going to be your teacher for this semester. You are all lucky!

Ss: Yeah!

T: Oh, by the way, I have someone to introduce to you. His name is Jerome and he is going to be your T.A. Do you have any questions for him or myself?

Ss: (silent)

T: By the way do you have the Interchange book? It's writing class today. Before we start, does somebody want to tell me about synonyms? What are they? Bring out your dictionaries and find out if you don't know. Oh, **you are more than welcome to bring in any kind of dictionary** [1]; electronic or book. It doesn't matter.

S1: It is similar? Same meaning in different use of word?

T: Excellent. Can someone give me an example?

S2: School and academy.

T: Perfect! They are different words that have the same meaning. That is what a synonym is. OK? Do you have pens and papers? Bring them out. We are going to write. Anybody want to write anything in particular?

S3: About the liberty.

T: Try to speak in full sentences like, "I want to write about our liberty."

S3: OK. I want to write about our liberty.

Tip Origin of Encyclopedia

The Greek word from which we get encyclopedia is made up of three words that mean 'in', 'a circle', and 'education'. So an encyclopedia is a collection of writing that deals with all subjects that lie with the circle, or boundaries of education. (그리스 어에서 유래된 '백과사전'은 '안', '원', '교육'이라는 세 단어로 구성되었다. 그래서 백과사전은 범위 안에, 또는 교육의 영역 안에 있는 모든 주제를 다루는 자료의 집합이다.)

Expressions used

1) **You are more than welcome to bring in any kind of dictionary**: This is a very polite and nice expression. We usually say 'I don't mind if you bring in your dictionary'. 이것은 매우 공손하고 멋진 표현이다. 대개 '어떤 사전을 가져와도 상관없다'고 표현한다.

Missilex

미사일 연습

 군사 훈련 및 브리핑에서 흔히 사용되는 'exercise'가 복합어로 사용될 경우 'ex'로 축약되어 사용된다는 점을 설명하고 있다.

T: Today we will be looking at a real military briefing. So, who knows what MISSILEX means?

S1: Missile? Shooting? Training?

T: Close.[1] MISSILEX means a Missile Excercise.

S1: Wow! A Missile Excercise.

T: If you want to move this desk, call it DESKEX. Then, what would I say if I wanted to move this chart.

S1: It is a CHARTEX.

T: Perfect. **This took me almost an hour to brief.**[2]

 Tip Origin of 'Tank'

The word, 'tank' was coined during World War I as a secret code name for the newly invented military vehicle. The name was kept when the vehicle eventually went into battle.
('탱크'는 1차대전 중 새롭게 발명된 군사용 차량에 대한 암호로 만들어졌다. 그 차량이 마침내 전투에 나갔을 때 그 이름이 그대로 유지되었다.)

Expressions used

1) **Close** : Almost but not quite 비슷하지만 정답은 아니다.

2) **This took me almost an hour to brief** : it took me an hour to explain. 설명하는 데 한 시간이 걸렸다.

Photosynthesis

광합성

 'Photosynthesis'를 설명하는 두 가지 방법. 일반적으로 복합어의 경우 대개 원어민은 어휘를 해체하여 설명하는 경우가 많다. 반면 후자와 같이 단순한 사전적 정의는 의미 전달이 어려운 경우가 많다. 여기서 'Paul'은 원어민 선생님의 이름이다. 아래 두 개의 지문은 각기 다른 원어민이 같은 단어를 설명한 것으로 시사하는 바가 크다.

1) 어휘 해체

S1: Paul, what does photosynthesis mean?

Paul: Ah, photosynthesis. Before we check out the meaning, **let's try to figure it out from the word.**[1] What does photo mean?

S2: Picture?

Paul: Umm… Absolutely not!! **Any other guess?**[2]

S3: Maybe, light?

Paul: Booyah! It's light. And synthesis means making something. So what would photosynthesis mean?

S4: Making food from light!

Paul: Correct! Using this, we can learn the meaning of some words by breaking them up into pieces. For example, let's look at the word 'photograph'. We said photo means light. So, what does graph mean?

S5: I think it is drawing.

Greg: Yeah. It's a drawing from light! Now, you guys get it?

Ss: Yes.

Expressions used

1) **Let's try to figure it out from the word** : 'Figure it out' means trying to understand something or solve something. The teacher is telling the students that we will try to understand the meaning of the word by analyzing its parts. 'Figure it out'는 어떤 것을 이해하거나 해결하려고 노력하는 것을 의미한다. 선생님은 학생에게 그 단어의 각 부분을 분석하여 단어의 의미를 이해하려고 시도할 것이다라고 말하고 있다.

2) **Any other guess?** : Does any other student have a guess as to what the word means?
그 단어가 무엇을 의미하는지 추측해 볼 또 다른 학생이 있습니까?

2) 개념 정의

S1: Paul, what is photosynthesis? I've never heard of this kind of word before.

Paul: **You guys gotta be kidding!!** [1] I know that all of you have heard this word at least once in your life! Especially in your biology class.

S2: **Is it related with plants?** [2]

Paul: Yeah! As you can see from the sentence 'Photosynthesis is a multi-step process which absorbs sunlight and changes it into nutrients'. Therefore, photosynthesis is the process of plants using sunlight as the source of energy.

Ss: (The students talk.) What's the word in Korean?

Tip Photosynthesis

In green plants, leaves make food to nourish the plant. This process is called photosynthesis. The chlorophyll in the leaves uses a combination of carbon dioxide, water and light to make sugar. It then passes the sugar to the rest of the plant through tubes. (녹색 식물에서 잎은 식물에 영양분을 주기 위해서 식량을 만든다. 이 과정은 광합성이라고 불린다. 잎 속의 엽록소가 이산화탄소와 물과 빛의 화합물을 이용하여 설탕을 만든다. 그리고 그 설탕을 줄기를 통하여 식물의 나머지 부분에 전달한다.)

Expressions used

1) **You guys gotta' be kidding!!** : A common expression. It does not mean that the teacher thinks the students are trying to fool the teacher or play a joke. It's an expression of surprise in this case that the students don't know something very simple.
일상적인 표현이다. 선생님은 학생들이 자신을 놀리거나 농담을 한다는 의미로 사용한 것이 아니다. 그것은 학생들이 매우 간단한 것을 모른다는 놀람의 표시이다.

2) **Is it related with plants?** : Is it associated with or have anything to do with plants? 그것은 식물과 연관이 있거나 관계가 있습니까?

Photograph

앞의 'photosynthesis'와 마찬가지로 어휘 해체를 이용하여 'photograph'를 설명하고 있다. 특히 마지막 부분에 'photo cannon'에 대한 대화와 같이 학생들의 자발적인 참여가 학습 효과를 높이고 있다.

T: Now, everyone knows what photosynthesis means?

Ss: Yeah.

T: Usually, photo means light. Let's take a look at the word photograph. Photo is light and graph means picture or drawing. A drawing made of light. See? How simple!

S1 & S2: (silent)

S1: Paul, do you know the game 'Starcraft'?

T: Yep.

S2: There is a unit called 'Photo Cannon'.

T: Ah hah. Then what does it shoot?

S1 & S2: Light Ball!!

T: Now you guys know how it works.[1] Booyah!

Expressions used

1) **Now you guys know how it works:** In this instance 'You guys' means 'the students.' 'How it works' refers to the process of breaking a word down to its parts. Meaning of words can often happen this way. 여기에서 'You guys'는 학생들을 지칭하는 말이다. 'How it works' '어떤 방식인지'는 단어가 각 부분으로 해체되는 과정을 지칭한다. 단어들의 의미는 종종 이런 방식으로 발생된다.

Fokker

포커기

 선생님이 보여주는 사진 속의 비행기 이름을 확인하는 대화이다.
학생들이 유추를 통해 교과 활동에 참여하도록 유도하고 있다.

T: Now, look at this photo. Do you know what this is?

S: No, sir.

T: What does it look like?

S: It looks like a P3C.

T: Are you sure? Look again⋯ No, it's a Fokker.

S: Facker?

T: Not Facker! Fokker! **Got it?** [1]

S: Fokker!

T: Very good. Alright next.

Tip Origin of 'Tangerine'

Tangerines are a fruit like a small orange with a loose skin. They are named after the Moroccan port of Tangier, from where the fruit was originally imported to Europe. ('밀감'은 부드러운 껍질이 있는 작은 오렌지와 비슷한 과일이다. 그 단어는 모로코의 항구, 탕헤르에서 나온 말이다. 원래 이 항구로부터 유럽으로 그 과일이 수입되었다.)

Expressions used

1) **Got it?** : Do you understand? 이해하겠습니까?

Irrigate

관개하다

 먼저 학생들이 모르는 어휘에 대해 물어볼 때의 질문문을 문법에 맞게 수정한 뒤 질문한 어휘의 의미를 예를 들어 설명하고 있다.

T: If there's any word confusing, just ask me or Inkyu(T.A.'s name).

S1: What mean 'irrigate'?

T: Say it once again.

S1: What mean irrigate?

T: No, last time we learned how to ask questions in proper form. That should be, "What does 'irrigate' mean?" or "What's the meaning of the word irrigate?" Everyone, please don't forget. Alright?

Ss: Alright.

T: Irrigate means giving water to crops or something. For example, if something gets into your eyes what do you do?

S2: We blow it out.

T: **Well, that could be one way.**[1] You irrigate water on your eyes when something gets in them.

Expressions used

1) **that could be one way** : That is one possible solution to a problem, or the answer to a question.
그것도 문제를 해결하거나 질문에 답하는 한 가지 방법이다.

Sacrifice

희생

 '희생'(sacrifice)의 의미를 설명한 뒤, 이를 바탕으로 헌신(devotion)의 의미도 설명하고 있다. 'sacrifice'가 기반 지식(scaffolding)으로 이용되고 있다.

T: Sacrifice is a very important value, especially to servicemen like you guys. Sacrifice means that you devote yourself to something which is worth more than your life. You must be willing to die for it. Are you guys ready to sacrifice for your country?

Ss: Yes! We are ready! We are midshipmen and we can even die for our country.

T: Oh really? I am very happy to hear that! Also, take note of the word, 'devotion'. **It has a very similar meaning to 'sacrifice' and is used as often as the word 'sacrifice'.**[1]

Tip Secret and Secretary

The word 'secret' comes from the Latin 'secretus', meaning 'separate' or 'hidden'. 'Secretary' comes from the same source because it originally referred to a person who was entrusted with a secret. (단어 'secret'는 분리된 또는 감추어진을 의미하는 라틴어 'secretus'에서 유래한다. 'Secretary' (비서)도 어원이 같으며, 원래 비밀을 위임받은 사람을 지칭한다.)

Expressions used

1) **It has a very similar meaning to 'sacrifice' and is used as often as the word 'sacrifice'** : The word is synonymous with sacrifice. 그 단어는 'sacrifice'와 동의어이다.

Diarrhea

설사

네 명의 원어민 선생님에게 설사(diarrhea)를 학생들에게 설명하는 방법을 문의하자, 각각 자신들의 설명 방법을 기술하였다. 다음 각각의 설명 방법을 참고하면 가르치는 데 참고가 될 것이다.

* Definition in Dictionary

excessive frequency and looseness of bowel movement

....

1) Explain in very simple English. (단순한 언어로 묘사하기)

When they have a stomach problem and they have problems using the toilet, sometimes they have a 'water pooh'. Pooh is another name for dung which is used by kids.

2) Use the cause and result. (인과관계로 설명)

When you eat too much or have rotten food, your stomach is upset, and you constantly go to the washroom. Spoiled milk or a rotten banana or bad food cause 'this'. (with visual cues for using the toilet)

3) Use a word / synonym they already know. (연관어 / 유의어를 이용해 묘사하기)

I would use the word 'dung' which all the students know well. After that I would simply demonstrate the act of rushing back and forth to the bathroom with urgency.

4) **Provide the correct Korean word for the vocabulary with the help of other students because she doesn't know Korean. (우리말로 번역하기)**

diarrhea is 설사 in Korean.

Cookings

여러 가지 식품의 요리법에 관한 대화이다. 선생님이 각 조장(captain)들
에게 그룹별로 각 식품의 요리법을 신속히 찾아내도록 지시하고 있다.

T: Let's shift gear!

Ss: What's 'shift gear'?

T: It means to go to another area. Will everyone look at the
board, please? Those are sequence adverbs. First, next,
after that, then, finally. These are all interchangeable.
Alright. In your group. I want you to discuss the most
common cooking methods such as bake, roast, etc.
Now bake and roast are similar, yet different. The main
difference is that in baking you usually have dry food like
bread but roast is cooking something like meat. So, all of
you have to say cooking methods. For example, fish, we
have fry and···

S: Boil?

T: Exactly.

S: What is 새우 in English?

T: That would be shrimp; S.H.R.I.M.P. Alright.
Captains, **let's try to get over this quickly!**[1]
(Students pretend to work harder.)
Remember! Common cooking methods. Not unusual
cooking methods. Nothing like fried brains. **Something ev-
erybody knows about.**[2]

S: One thing??

Cookings

T: Not one thing. It could have many different cooking methods, right?

S: Right. But how about bananas?

T: You don't cook bananas, do you? You just eat it raw. Alright, let's review some answers here now. Are we ready?

S: Not yet.

T: I'll give you 1 more minute. James, what's up?

Jamese: Oh. OK.

T: Alright! Let's talk about fish!!

S: Fry, boil.

S2: Boil?

S: Like 매운탕.

S3: Oh yeah!

T: Excellent. Now for shrimp.

S: Boil, barbecue, fry!

T: Good. How about eggs?

S: Steam.

T: How about beef? We have roast, boil, and barbecue.

S: Steam?

T: That's not very common, is it?

Ss: Hahaha.

T: Wow! MinGi! Are you finished? That's great! You're so fast!

Mingi: Thank you very much.

T: **But you should think before you act.**[3] See?

Mingi: Oh! Sorry. Thank you for your attention.

Tip Sandwich

The sandwich is named after the 4th Earl of Sandwich, John Montagu(1718~92), who was so addicted to gambling that he never wanted to leave the gaming table. So when the Earl needed something to eat, a servant would bring him some cold beef, which he liked to have between two slices of bread. This snack soon came to be known as a sandwich.

(샌드위치라는 이름은 샌드위치 존 몬테규 백작 4세로부터 유래되었다. 그는 너무 게임에 중독이 되어 심지어 게임 테이블을 떠나려고 하지 않았다. 그래서 백작이 먹을 것이 필요할 때 하인은 그에게 두 개의 빵 조각 사이에 쇠고기 몇 점이 들어간 것을 주었다. 이 간식이 샌드위치로 알려지게 되었다.)

Expressions used

1) **let's try to get over this quickly!** : Let's try and cover this new teaching/learning material or activity quickly.
   이 학습 자료 또는 교과 활동을 빨리 진행하자.

2) **Something everybody knows about** : The teacher is telling the students to choose topics that all the other students will be familiar with so they are easy to talk about. 선생님이 학생들에게 다른 학생들이 잘 알고 이야기하기 쉬운 화제를 선택하도록 지시하고 있다.

3) **you should think before you act** : The teacher is telling the student that before he/she does something, he/she should think about it first. 행동하기 전에 먼저 생각해 보라고 학생에게 지시하고 있다.

[Cartoon] In A Restaurant

Bossy

 인간의 특성에 관련된 형용사에 대해 여러가지 설명을 하고 있다. 학생들의 대답이 단편적이고, 질문이 비문법적(ungrammatical)이어서 대화가 자연스럽게 진행되지 못하고 있다.

T: What does 'mean' mean?

S1: Bad meaning.

T: Bad meaning, yes.

S2: Like 'cruel'.

T: Yes, what is the opposite of 'mean'?

S3: Kind.

T: Exactly.

S3: How about 'bossy'. **I don't know 'bossy'** [1]

T: The meaning 'bossy' comes from the word 'boss'. Do you know 'boss'? He is in charge of the group. At work, he sometimes makes you do things, open the window, get him a coffee, and so on.

S3: **This telling means this meaning like the order?** [2]

T: It is kind of ordering, yes.

S4: Is there any difference between obsessive and stubborn?

T: Obsessive means when you do something, you can't stop. You concentrate on one thing. Stubborn means you never change your mind, so there's a little bit of a difference. Similar but different.

Bossy

으시대는

 Origin of 'Coffee'

'Café' is the French word for 'coffee' or 'coffee house' and is usually spelled with an acute accent on the 'e', that is, é. ('Café'는 '커피' or '커피점'을 의미하는 불어이며, 대개 'e' 위에 양음 악센트가 있는 é로 쓴다.)

Expressions used

1) **I don't know 'bossy'** : I don't know what the word 'bossy' means.
   'bossy'의 의미를 모르겠습니다.

2) **This telling means this meaning like the order?** : The student's poor attempt to say in English. "Bossy means a person who likes to give a lot of orders to other people."
   학생들이 서툴게 영어로 질문하려고 하고 있다. "'지배적인(Bossy)'이라는 말은 다른 사람들에게 많은 지시를 내리기 좋아하는 사람을 의미한다."

Skyscraper

Skyscraper

Unit 19

고층 건물

'고층 건물(high-rise)'과 '현재(present)'의 동의어를 묻고 있다. 선생님이 동의어에 대해 묻는 간단한 질문문이 참고할 만하다.

T: What's a high-rise?

S: Umm, building?

T: Yeah, it's a building, but what building?

S: High building.

T: Yes, a high-rise is a very tall building. Then, **what is another name for it?**[1]

S: Skysc…

T: Skyscraper!

T: Now, **what kinds of words do we use for 'present'?**[2]

S1: Now!

T: Absolutely! **And what else?**[3]

S2: Nowadays.

S3: Today.

T: Great. Nowadays and today.

S4: These days.

T: I like 'these days'. Good job, kids.

Skyscraper

Tip Ground Floor vs First Floor

In the US, the ground floor of a house is called the first floor. To the British, the first floor is the one above the ground floor, which Americans call the second floor. (미국에서는 집의 '바닥층'을 '1층'이라고 한다. 영국인에게 '1층'은 바닥층 위에 있는 층으로, 미국인들은 '2층'이라고 부른다.)

Expressions used

1) **What is another name for it?** : The teacher is asking for a synonym. 선생님은 동의어를 묻고 있다.

2) **What kinds of words do we use for 'present'?** : Asking for synonyms for the word 'present.' 'present'의 동의어를 묻고 있다.

3) **And what else?** : Asking for more examples or synonyms. 또 다른 예나 동의어를 묻고 있다.

Memorial Day

추모일에 하는 행동 및 무장구보에 대한 이야기이다. 학생들이 '묵념', '무장구보' 등의 정확한 표현을 모르고 있다.

T: Will you come to school on Monday?

S: No. Memorial Day.

T: Who are we going to remember on Memorial Day?

S: 60 American veterans will come to our museum.

T: Oh, really? Did anyone of your grandfathers fight during the Korean War?

S: His cousin's grandfather did. (Pointing to a student.)

T: What do you do on Memorial Day?

S: (묵념을 영어로 뭐라 하지? 고개를 숙이는 모습을 취한다.)

T: Hold your head down. We call it a moment of silence.…

T: What did you do last week?

S: Full bag training.

T: **Full equipment training.** [1] Is that a punishment?

S: No, just training.…

T: **Did everyone remember that we have a quiz today?** [2] Please put everything away. Ali and Sunny, put your books away. Write your names on the paper. John, can you read the directions for us?

Memorial Day

추모일

Expressions used

1) **Full equipment training** : Military training carrying a full back pack and other equipment. 완전군장. 배낭을 가득 채우고 다른 장비도 함께 운반하는 군사훈련.

2) **Did everyone remember that we have a quiz today?** : The students were told (probably in the previous class) that there will be a quiz. The teacher is asking the students if the students remember. 학생들은 (아마 이전 시간에) 시험이 있을 것이라는 것을 들었다. 선생님은 학생들에게 기억하고 있는지 묻고 있다.

Gross & Net

두 단어의 의미 차이를 간단한 예를 들어 설명하고 있다. 학생의 'gross'(총액)의 의미를 묻는 질문에, 이를 기반(scaffolding)으로 하여 선생님은 'net'(실수령액)까지 같이 설명한다.

T: Now we've been talking about the top 10 money making movies. But **these movies are ranked just by the gross amount.**[1]

S1: **What do you mean, gross?**[2]

T: Ah. Okay. Let's take a look at these two words. (Writing 'gross' and 'net' on the board) 'Gross' means just the money you make. For example, you earn $500 per month. That's your gross salary. However, actually you get less money than that because of the taxes. So, **you get around $430 something.**[3] That's the net amount of your salary.

Ss: Ah.

T: So, 'Titanic', which ranked first, may not be first by net amount because it cost really a huge amount of money to film that movie. Got it?

Gross & Net

총액과 순이익

Tip 'Equivalent to' vs 'Equivalent of'
You can use the word 'to' with the adjective 'equivalent': That's equivalent to $10. With 'equivalent' as a noun, use the word 'of': That's the equivalent of $10. (형용사 'equivalent(동등한)' 은 전치사 'to'를 수반한다. : 그것은 10달러에 상당한다. 명사로서 'equivalent(동등한 가치)'는 'of'를 사용한다. : 그 것은 10달러의 가치가 있다.)

Expressions used

1) **these movies are ranked just by the gross amount**: The teacher is telling the students that the list of the most profitable movies is based on gross amount, not net amount.
   선생님은 학생들에게 가장 수익이 많은 영화 목록은 순이익이 아닌, 총액을 기준으로 만들어졌다고 말한다.

2) **What do you mean, gross?**: The student is asking what the word 'gross' means. 'gross(총액의)'의 의미가 무엇인지 묻고 있다.

3) **you get around $430 something**: Somewhere close to $430; maybe a little more, maybe a little less.
   430달러 정도. 아마 조금 더 많거나, 조금 더 적거나.

[Cartoon] At the Bank

Grocery Store

식품점의 개념에 대한 설명이다. 질문 방법에 대한 참고 자료이다. 첫 번째 질문을 이해하지 못하자 두 번째 질문으로 바꾸어 물었으며 (rephrase), 세 번째는 보다 단순화된 질문(simplification)으로 학생들의 대답을 유도하고 있다.

T: **What's a grocery store?**[1]

S: (Faces the teacher⋯)

T: Then, what do you buy in a grocery store?

S: Groceries.

T: What are 'groceries'?

S: Food and⋯

T: Yeah, food and the things that we need in our homes. Things like soap, toothpaste, etc. Woori-Mart is a grocery store.

Tip Export vs Import

Exports are sent to and sold in another country, while imports are bought from another country to sell in your own country. (수출은 다른 나라로 보내어 팔리는 것이고, 수입은 다른 나라에서 사들 어서 자국에 파는 것이다.)

Expressions used

1) **What's a grocery store?**: The teacher is asking the students to define grocery store (as compared to other types of stores).
선생님은 다른 유형의 상점과 비교하여) 학생들에게 잡화점을 정의하라고 요구하고 있다.

Fun & Funny

'재미있는'과 '우스운'

 'Fun'과 'Funny'의 의미 차이에 대한 설명이다. '노인과 바다'의 독후감을 통해 두 단어의 의미 차이를 구분하고 있다.

T: Did you read the book, 'The Old Man and the Sea'?

S: Yes, I did.

T: Was it fun or funny?

S: It was funny!

T: It was funny?

S: Yeah, funny.

T: Okay, listen carefully. 'Fun' and 'funny' do not have the same meaning. **They are not the same.**[1] 'Funny': When you make a joke or something makes you laugh, that's funny. 'Fun': When you are doing something that you really enjoy doing, like playing soccer or another game, that's 'fun'. You don't have to laugh for something to be fun. Alright?

S: Yeah. It was fun.

Expressions used

1) **They are not the same**: They don't have the same meaning.
그것들은 같은 의미가 아니다.

Monument & Statue

기념비와 조각상

 기념비와 조각상의 의미 차이에 대한 설명이다. 학생의 공손하지 못한 질문(impolite question) 방법을 수정한 뒤에, 질문에 대답하고 있다.

S1: What is monument?

T: Hey, listen up! When you don't know the meaning of a word, usually how should you ask?

S1: Hmm… What means…?

Ss: Meaning.

T: No. You know that the question wasn't a complete sentence. When you ask you have to say, "What does ____ mean?" Alright?

Ss: Alright!

S1: Sir, what does 'monument' mean?

T: Perfect! Your question was perfect. Well, monument can be any structure which was built so we remember something. For instance, The Douglas McArthur Statue in Incheon. It remembers the Incheon landing during the Korean War.

S2: Then, is there a difference a statue and a monument?

T: Yeah. The statue can be a part of monument. **However, a statue doesn't always cause us to remember something.**[1] Got it?

S2: Got it!!

Monument & Statue 기념비와 조각상

Expressions used

1) **However, a statue doesn't always cause us to remember something** : The teacher is explaining to the students the difference between a statue and a monument. A monument is erected (built) so that people will remember or honor an event in history. A statue, on the other hand, isn't usually made in order for people to remember or honor an event. 선생님은 조각상과 기념비와의 차이를 학생들에게 설명하고 있다. 기념비는 사람들이 역사적인 사건을 기억하거나 기리기 위해 세워진다. 반면, 조각상은 반드시 사건을 기억하거나 기리기 위해 만들어지는 것은 아니다.

Brother & Sister

남자 형제와 여동생

 한국과 미국의 문화적 차이에 따른 'Brother'와 'sister' 그리고 'lover'의 의미 차이를 설명하고 있다.

T: Does anyone know the actual definition of brother and sister?

Ss: Yes.

S1: We call brother and sister in family.

T: Good, but what about a person not family but older or younger than you; do we call them a brother or sister in Korea?

S2: Yes. Why not?

T: Haha, I thought you would say that. In Korean culture, it is perfectly right, but in English culture brother or sister is only someone that is related to you; family. Understand? Do you understand now?

Ss: Yes, we understand.

T: **Same as that, if you are in a relationship, you will say 'lover' in Korea.**[1] Lover means sex partner. Unless you are going to marry him or her, it's a boyfriend or a girlfriend. General friends are just friends. Got it?

S1: Can you say male friend and female friend?

T: Very good questions. Yes, those can be said.

T: Alright, as you can see, **there are different cultures**

between Korea and the West. [2] I personally think that conversation class is a good opportunity to speak correctly according to the appropriate culture.

Tip Sexism

Watch out for sexism in your writing. Many people now object to the use of 'he' and 'his' when what is really meant is 'he or she' and 'his or hers'. One way round this is to use 'they' or 'their'.: 'If a student is unsure how to register, they should ask their tutor.' You can also easily avoid male-sounding words, for example by using 'the human race' or 'humans' for 'mankind', etc. (여러분의 글에서 성차별을 조심하십시오. 오늘날 많은 사람들은 'he or she' 그리고 'his or hers'의 의미로 'he'와 'his'를 사용하는 것을 반대합니다. 이것을 피하는 한 가지 방법은 'they'나 'their'를 사용하는 것입니다.; '학생이 기록하는 방법을 모르면 학업 지도 선생님에게 물으세요. 또한 'mankind'[인간] 대신 'the human race' or 'humans'를 사용하면 남성적인 어휘를 쉽게 피할 수 있습니다.

Expressions used

1) **Same as that, if you are in a relationship, you will say 'lover' in Korea** : Similar to the way Koreans use 'brother' and 'sister', they also use the word 'lover' differently or even incorrectly. 한국인이 'brother'와 'sister'라는 말을 사용하는 것과 마찬가지로, 'lover'도 다르게 심지어는 잘못 사용한다.

2) **there are different cultures between Korea and the West** : Western culture and Korean culture are different. 서양 문화와 한국 문화는 다르다.

Cloth & Clothes

'천'과 '의복'

 유사한 단어의 발음 차이에 대한 설명이다. 여기서는 학생들이 잘 구분하지 못하는, [ð]([z]에 가까운 유성음)와 [θ]([s]에 가까운 무성음)의 구별에 대한 설명을 하고 있다.

T: Pronounce the following words; cloth and clothes.

S1: Cloth.

T: Those are the common pronunciation problems for the Korean students. 'Cloth.' This is the material such as silk, cotten, wool, etc. Repeat after me, 'cloth!'

S1: Cloth.

T: Now, 'clothes.' **It sounds like [cloz], not the [th] sound, such as pants, shirts, etc.** [1] Those are clothes. Repeat after me, 'clothes'.

S1: Clothes.

T: Alright! Now, read the book.

S2: (While students are reading the paragraph.) The traditional clothes [kloθs].

T: Would you repeat that word again?

S2: Clothes [kloθs].

T: No, no, no. You don't pronounce it as [kloθs], but as [klouðz]. Most Koreans get confused when pronouncing this word because when we say it without the '-es' the 'th' sound becomes [θ]. And the important thing that you guys have to keep in mind is that clothes is just one word. It's also an uncountable noun just like the chalk which we mentioned couple of minutes ago.

Cloth & Clothes

Tip Origin of 'Tire'

'Tire' comes from the word, 'attire'(clothing), because it was thought of as the clothing of a wheel. And the fitting of tire to wheels was once known as 'shoeing'. ('Tire'[타이어]는 'attire'[옷을 입다]라는 단어에서 유래된 것이다. 왜냐하면 그것은 바퀴의 옷이라고 생각했기 때문이다. 바퀴에 타이어를 맞추는 것을 한때는 '구두를 신기다'라고 했다.)

Expressions used

1) **It sounds like [cloz], not the [th] sound, such as pants, shirts, etc.** : The teacher is trying to explain the correct pronunciation and meanings of the words 'clothes' and 'cloth'. 선생님이 'clothes'와 'cloth'의 올바른 발음과 의미를 설명하고 있다.

[Cartoon] Selling

Marching & Parade

'행진'과 '행렬'

 일반적인 군에서의 행진(marching)과 행사에서의 행렬(parade)의 의미 차이에 대해 설명하고 있다.

T: This was a very busy week for the stndents. It is always busy for you guys but this week was extra busy.

S3: There was a parade.

T: Not a parade… what do you call it? What is a parade exactly?

Ss: Marching.

S1: What is the difference between marching and parade?

T: Usually, when a parade is in your country, it's in Seoul with everybody walking and waving. What you're doing is marching, just the walking. I know frequently that you have ceremonies, but why were you marching yesterday?

S3: Changing the captain of the midshipmen.

T: Who is the new captain of the midshipmen?

S2: Admiral Son.

T: What did you hear about this new guy, such as his personality or style?

S5: He has a very good leadership.

T: So he is a strong leader?

S4: He is a gentleman.

S1: Cool guy.

T: Eric, what did you say?

S6: He is a brave man.

Marching & Parade '행진'과 '행렬'

T: Good, so you're expecting to have a good captain this semester. However, I heard that **you had some problem with this marching.**[1]

S3: One of the officers said that this was the worst ceremony in the history of the ceremony.

T: First of all, anybody guilty of this mistake?

(3 students raise hands.)

S4: I have some part of the fault, but our junior flag carrier⋯ 뭐라고 해야 되지.

S2: (After looking up the computer) He was belated.

T: You mean he was too late?

S1: They were all late.

T: Why were they all late?

S1: One of them forgot his pin, but they are one team, so they all waited for him. But the problem is that our troop already going through the ground, but they didn't be there.

T: What did they do when they arrived?

S1: They just pretended nothing problem. They were just walking there.

T: So what happened after the ceremony?

S4: Haha⋯ Our staff and our leaders had to prepare the

food. And we had to running on the ground. Not everybody, but just the leaders.

T: Who also had to run?

S7: Me, 2nd company chief.

T: The reason you were punished was because of this one
guy?

S4: No, because all of them, as a team.

T: I think **that is very military thinking.** [2] I think only it was
one person's mistake.

S4: More important thing was that there were many other
mistakes besides that.

T: Besides being late?

S1: Yes, a lot.

Expressions used

1) **you had some problem with this marching** : 'Marching' is used as a
noun (gerund). So, there was a problem with how well the students
marched. 'marching'이 명사로 사용되었다. 그래, 학생들의 분열에 문제가 생겼다.

2) **that is very military thinking** : The teacher is saying that the
response is typical of the way military people think.
선생님은 그 반응이 전형적으로 군인들이 생각하는 방식이라고 말하고 있다.

Greedy & Arrogant

'욕심 많은'과 '오만한'

 형용사 어휘 연습에서 선생님이 'greedy'와 'arrogant'의 의미를 묻고 있다.

T: Do you all know what it means to be greedy? **How about being arrogant?** [1]

S1: I know what it means greedy, but arrogant, I don't know.

S2: I know the meaning of both and I can explain them.

T: Alright, then go ahead!

S2: Being greedy is to be selfish and not to share with other people. For example, Mr. Kim is greedy. He never shares food with midshipmen.

Ss: Hahahahaha.

S2: Also, being arrogant is to be showing bad attitude. It is ignoring other people.

T: Well explained. To add a bit more to your excellent explanation, to be arrogant is to demonstrate ignorant behavior to others, provoking them by being naughty.

Expressions used

---

1) **How about being arrogant?** : The teacher is asking what the word 'arrogant' means. 선생님은 '오만한'의 의미를 묻고 있다.

'What's the problem?'
& 'What's your problem?' '별일 없어?'와 '불만이 뭐니?'

 먼저 교과서를 지참하지 않은 학생을 훈계한 다음, 일상생활에서 혼돈하기 쉬운 2개 관용 표현의 의미를 학생과의 대화를 통해 알기 쉽게 설명하고 있다.

T: Who has not brought their book?

S1: I didn't.

T: Why? Do you have any good reason so?

S1: I am sorry. I forgot.

T: I am not here to tell you off, but it is principle. It shows your attitude towards class. Next time, please don't forget to bring it. As I remind you many times, be prepared and organized. Right? It's for your own benefit.

Ss: Yes, John.

T: Homework, preparing for classes, these are invisible promises between teacher and students.

T: OK. I want to talk about the issue on 'problem'. **The word, 'problem' can be docked with many common sentences.**[1] Anybody brave enough to give an example?

S1: Hmm, I have many secret problems.

T: Good! Today I want to distinguish between two similar sentences that have completely different meanings. What's different between, "What's the problem?" and "What's your problem?"

S2: Are they not the same meaning like, "How are you?"

T: Good attempt. What else?

Ss: (silent)

T: Listen carefully and write the notes down in your notebook. It is very important when you go or travel overseas. First, the meaning of "What's the problem?" is to ask someone how they feel. It's same as "Are you OK?"

S3: So it's like, "What's the matter?"

T: Got it, perfect! Everybody knew it already, right?

Ss: Of course.

T: Cool, then what about, "What's your problem?" If you translate directly to Korean, it could also be, "What's your matter?" But it is not. You say, "What's your problem?" when somebody bothers or irritates you. If one of the students hits me on the shoulder and walks away without saying "Sorry" or "Excuse me", I can say, "Hey, what's your problem?" Understood?

Ss: Aha! We get it now.

T: OK, so don't you say to your friend who is crying and seems to be having a bad day, "Hey, what's your problem?" Instead you should politely ask, "What's the problem?"

Ss: OK, John! Thank you.

Expressions used

1) **The word, 'problem' can be docked with many common sentences**: The teacher is using the word 'docked' to mean connected.
선생님은 'docked'(결합된)라는 단어를 '연결된'이라는 의미로 사용하고 있다.

Status quo

그저 그래

 인사말에 대한 대답으로 'Nothing Special' 대신에 동의어인 'Status quo'
를 사용하여 학생들의 질문을 유도하고 있다.

T: So, how are you doing?

S1: No, something special.

T: Ah. There's nothing special that happened to you
today? Actually, it's better to say nothing special than no
something special. Got it?

S1: Okay. Nothing special happened.

T: Status quo.

Ss: Satus… What?

T: Satus quo. (Writing the word on the blackboard)

S2: What does 'status quo' mean?

T: Nice, **I was waiting for that question.**[1] 'Status quo' means
nothing bad nor nothing good has happened. **Everything
is as just as it should be.**[2] Status quo!

Ss: Status quo!

Expressions used

1) **I was waiting for that question:** The teacher was expecting that
eventually a student would ask that particular question.
선생님은 마침내 학생이 그 질문을 하기를 기대하고 있었다.

2) **Everything is as just as it should be:** This is the definition of the
term 'status quo'. 이것이 그 단어 'status quo'(평상시와 다름없어)의 의미이다.

Get down to

 선생님은 학생들이 수업 시간에 '질문'을 하지 않는다는 점을 지적하고 질문을 유도하고 있다. 그리고 'start' 대신 'get down to(시작하다)'를 의도적으로 사용해 학생들의 질문을 유도하여 수업 활동을 진행하고 있다.

T: Good morning class!

S1: Good morning, sir!

T: Alright! Did everyone do their homework?

S1: Yes, we finish.

T: You should say 'finished' because it's past tense, right?

S1: Oh! My mistake.

T: OK. Let's go through it, shall we?

S: Yes! ⋯

(After reviewing homework)

T: Good work, everyone! **There is one thing that is missing from you guys.**[1]

S2: Huh? What is it?

T: You guys never ask me questions.

S3: Um, well, we are perfect?

T: Hahaha! No, even I make mistakes. You don't have to be shy! Look around you. All of you are here to learn English right?

Ss: Right.

T: Then, go ahead! Any questions?

S3: I have a question! What 'tranquility' mean? I look up dictionary and I still don't understand.

T: First of all, it's 'looked up in the dictionary' because it's past tense. You didn't do it just now, right?

S3: Yes. I did it yesterday.

T: And secondly, 'tranquility' means calmness, peace, and quiet. It must have confused you. Now you should know what tranquility is used for.

S3: Wow! Now I understand! Thank you.

T: I'm glad I could be of service. You guys are so enthusiastic. I really enjoy teaching.

S4: You are a good teacher! You explain really well.

T: Thank you, but enough chatting. Let's get down to business shall we?

Ss: OK.

S5: Greg, what does 'get down to business' mean?

T: Great! I thought you'd never ask. 'Getting down to business' means to do or finish what you are supposed to do.

S6: So, you mean 'finish work'?

T: Close but homework, you do it alone right? Unless you copy each other….

Ss: Yes….

T: You say 'let's get down to business' when more than two people are on the same task. For example, what do you guys and I do when we meet each other?

S5: We study English!

T: Bingo! So, what would 'getting down to business' mean for us?

Ss: Study English!

T: **There you go.**[2]

S5: Now we understand!

T: Great! One by one, step by step, you guys are getting better and better. Someday you might even speak better English than me!

S6: **We wish we can do that.**[3]

Ss: (laughs) Hahahaha….

Expressions used

1) **There is one thing that is missing from you guys**:The teacher is commenting that there is always something missing in class:the students never seem to ask questions. 선생님은, 수업에서 항상 빠진 것이 있으며, 그것은 학생들이 질문을 하지 않는 것 같다는 점을 언급하고 있다.

2) **There you go**:In this case, the teacher told the student that his/her answer was correct. 이 경우에는 학생에게 그의 답이 옳다는 것을 말한다.

3) **We wish we can do that**:The student is commenting that he/she wishes that someday they can speak English as well as or better than the teacher. 학생들이 그들도 언젠가 선생님보다 영어를 더 잘 혹은 그만큼 하고 싶다고 언급하고 있다.

Beats Me

몰라

 여름 방학 계획에 대해 나누던 대화 중에 선생님이 'beat me'라는 관용
어를 사용하여 질문을 유도하고 있다.

T: Hey, everyone. It's summer already. What do you like the
most about summer?

Ss: Summer vacation.

T: Haha! You're right. **I can't wait, too.**[1]

S1: Do you have any special plan for the vacation?

T: Beats me. I haven't thought about it yet.

Ss: Beats me? What do you mean? We didn't beat you up.
We would never do such a thing.

T: Nononono. Haha! 'Beats me' means I have no idea. I have
no clue what I'm going to do on summer vacation.

Ss: Aha! We got it!

Tip Usage of Exclamation mark

An exclamation mark(!) is used at the end of sentences that express a strong command (Get
out of here!) or surprise (What an extraordinary idea!). It is also used for warnings (Look out!) and
after interjections (Ouch!). (느낌표는 문장 끝에서 강한 명령[여기서 나가!], 놀람[얼마나 놀라운 아이디어인
가!], 경고[조심해!], 감탄사[아야!] 다음에 사용된다.)

Expressions used

1) **I can't wait, too** : In other words, we can say : I'm looking forward
to it, too ; I can't wait to go ; I know. 다른 말로 '나도 역시 기다리고 있다', '무
척 즐기고 싶다', '(그 심정) 나도 알지'라고 표현할 수도 있다.

Night Owl

야간에 일하는 사람

 수업 전에 다수의 학생들이 엎드려 자고 있기 때문에, 선생님은 그 이유를 묻고 그 상황에 연관된 관용구를 사용하여 대화를 유도하고 있다.

T: Good morning, everyone! What a beautiful day, isn't it?

Ss: (No answer, everyone sleeping)

T: Wow. What happened here? What did you guys do last night?

Ss: We have a science test next period. It's really hard and covers almost every chapter in the book. We spent all night studying for it and went to bed at four am.

T: Didn't you go to bed at three am two days ago? What was that for?

Ss: Oh, that was for a history exam.

T: Sounds like you are night owls.

Ss: A night owl? Isn't it an animal? The one with huge eyes and brown feather?

T: That's right! Owls are nocturnal animal. They sleep during the day and stay up all night like you guys.

Ss: Oh, come on. Give us a break.

Tip Hibernation vs Sleeping

Animals hibernate during the cold, winter months when food is scarce. They eat as much as they can before finding a safe place to curl up for the winter. Hibernation isn't the same as sleeping, though. Sleeping takes more energy than hibernation. To conserve energy, the breathing and heartbeat of a hibernating animal slows down so much that they may appear to be almost dead. (동물들은 식량이 부족한 추운 겨울 몇 달간 동면을 한다. 그들은 겨울 동안 웅크리고 잘 수 있는 안전한 장소를 찾기 전에 가능한 한 많이 먹어둔다. 그러나 동면은 잠과 다르다. 잠은 동면보다 더 많은 에너지가 소비된다. 에너지를 보존하기 위해서 동면하는 동물들의 호흡과 심장 박동은 아주 느려져서 거의 죽은 것처럼 보인다.)

Butterflies in the Stomach

불안하다

 영어 구두 시험을 앞두고 초조해 하는 학생들의 마음을 관용구로 나타내고 이를 이용하여 담화를 이어가고 있다.

T: Hello, everyone. How are you?

Ss: Not so good….

T: Yes? And why is that? It seems like something terrible has happened to you.

Ss: We have an English final exam later today. We have to have a conversation in English. It's about 20% of our final grade, so it's very important. No matter how much we prepare and practice, we still feel nervous.

T: Ah hah! You guys have butterflies in stomach.

Ss: Butterflies in what? We don't have any butterflies in our stomach. We ate chicken for lunch.

T: Haha! That's not what I meant. Having 'butterflies in the stomach' means you are extremely nervous. Think about it. If you had butterflies in your stomach for real, what would it feel like?

Ss: It's hard to imagine, but it would be very yucky and unpleasant. We might throw up.

T: Exactly! Don't you feel the same way when you are extremely nervous?

Ss: Oh, yeah. You're right! We do feel like having butterflies in our stomach.

[Cartoon] The Air Show

형용사와 관용구를 학습하는 과정에서 이루어진 담화이다. 개념 설명 후 단어를 개인에게 적용하여 내용에 대한 이해를 확인하는 방법을 써 수 업을 효율적으로 진행하고 있다. 학생들에게 먼저 의미를 묻고 설명하는 방식으로 어휘를 학습시키고 있다. 반면 후반에는 학생들의 질문에 답하 는 형식으로 진행하고 있다.

T: Do you know these words, strict and stubborn?

S1: I don't know 'stubborn'.

T: Stubborn, it's really a negative word. [1] (She writes 'stubborn' on the board.) People who are stubborn never change their mind. They're always right and they never change their mind. So are you stubborn, Jake?

S1: No.

T: What do you call a woman whose husband has died? What do we call her?

S1: Solo.

Ss: Haha.

T: If you are a woman and your husband dies, you are called a widow. And if you are a man and your wife dies, you are called a widower.

T: What does this expression 'catch up' mean?

S1: Ketchup?

T: Not ketchup, catch up.

S2: Chase something?

T: OK, **'to catch up' means when you haven't seen someone for a long time, you want to catch up with him.** [2] You want to hear about what had happened during that time.

S1: It means to know someone?

T: Yes, because we haven't seen each other for a long time. ··· Insu, why are you quiet?

S1: He break his girlfriend.

T: Not break.

S2: Break up.

T: So you broke up with your girlfriend. Why?

Insu: **It wasn't a good match.**[3] She's going to um···.

T: After university, right?

S1: Yes.

T: **Does anyone know that in English?**[4] ··· OK. It's graduate school. So she's in graduate school to study violin?

S1: Yes, ma'am.

T: Any word you don't understand?

S1: Conceited.

T: It means you think you are better than anybody else.

S2: Bully.

T: 'Bully' is someone who threatens. What does it mean to threaten?

S2: Too aggressive.

T: OK, bully, these are the people who start fights, who bully people. Any other word you don't understand?

S1: Grumpy.

T: They are always in a bad mood. Never smiling, never happy. Do we have any grumps here?

Ss: No.

T: No. Everyone's happy?

S3: What is gossip?

T: **A gossip is someone who spreads rumors.** [5] Someone who always talks about other people. Who is a gossip here?

S4: Mooch.

T: A mooch is someone who always borrows something but never returns it. A moocher says, "Oh, can I please borrow some money? I'll return it to you tomorrow." But they never give it back. Stingy people are very cheap, like Scrooge.

S1: I don't know what ritual means.

T: Well, a ritual is kind of a ceremony. Hmm, like when at Chuseok you go to your ancestor's grave, cut the grass and **set the table for the ceremony.** [6] Those kinds of work are what we call a ritual. Ritual is an established procedure for a religious rite.

Practicing Words

어휘 연습

Expressions used

1) **Stubborn, it's really a negative word**: The word 'stubborn' usually has a negative meaning. '완고한'은 대개 부정적인 의미를 지닌다.

2) **'to catch up' means when you haven't seen someone for a long time, you want to catch up with him.**: The teacher is explaining the idiom 'catch up'. In this case, 'catch up' means to speak to someone you haven't seen for a long time and find out what he/she has been doing since last they met. 선생님이 'catch up' (따라잡다, 만회하다)라는 관용어를 설명하고 있다. 이 경우 'catch up'은 당신이 오랫동안 만나지 못한 사람에게 그동안의 근황을 알아본다는 의미이다.

3) **It wasn't a good match**: The student is saying that he and his girlfriend were not a good couple. They didn't have much in common. 그와 그의 여자친구는 어울리는 한 쌍이 아니라고 학생이 말하고 있다. 그들은 공통점이 없다.

4) **Does anyone know that in English?**: Does anyone know how to say that word or expression in English? 누가 그 단어나 표현을 영어로 나타내는 방법을 알고 있나요?

5) **A gossip is someone who spreads rumors**: The teacher is explaining the noun form of the word 'gossip' as someone who hears a rumor about someone and quickly tells that rumor to other people. 명사 'gossip'을, 누군가에 대한 소문을 듣고 그 소문을 재빨리 다른 사람에게 말하는 사람으로써 설명하고 있다.

6) **set the table for the ceremony**: 'Set the table' means to put plates, cups, knives, forks, etc. on the table to prepare for a meal. '식탁을 차리다'는 식사를 준비하기 위해서 식탁에 접시, 컵, 칼, 포크 등을 두는 것을 의미한다.

Practicing Idioms

 관용어 교재('All clear')에서 이미 학습한 관용어를 반복, 개념 정의, 적용 등 다양한 방법으로 복습하고 있다.

T: (After explaining what 'doing on my own' means to students)

I can iron my clothes on my own. Repeat after me; I can iron my clothes on my own.

Ss: I can iron my clothes on my own.

T: Excellent!

T: Next, I am just about to do something! What does this mean?

Ss: Be ready to do something?

T: Good! It's easy!

T: Are you burnt out? [1]

Ss: Yes!

T: Really? Why?

Ss: Because we have too much homework.

T: Wow. OK! Your homework is to write two sentences using each idiom!

Expressions used

1) **Are you burnt out?** : Are you exhausted?; Are you overworked?; Are you overly tired? 너무 과로했니? 너무 피곤하니?

Reviewing Idioms

관용어의 복습

 지난 시간에 관용어 교재('All clear')에서 이미 학습한 아래 여섯 개의 관용어를 개념을 통해 찾아내는 연습을 하고 있다.

T: Now, a little bit of review. Close your books.

[Idioms which the students learned last class]

- **[get, have] cold feet** : become so nervous about starting something new
- **be dying to do something** : want to do something very, very much
- **in common** : shared together or equally
- **finished** : done, through
- **hang on** : to continue listening [or waiting] on the phone
- **good luck** : used to say when you wish that (s)he will be successful

....

T: You are very nervous about doing something. (Designating a student)
S1: Cold feet.
T: You're really, really want to do something.
S2: Try to do.
T: Similar.
S3: Dying for something.
T: Finished?

S4: Through.

T: Do you like girls?

S5: Yes.

T: Me, too. Do you like movies?

S5: Yes.

T: Me, too. We like the same things. We have⋯

S5: We have a lot in common.

T: **What if I want you to wait on the phone?** [1]

S6: Hang on.

T: I'm going to do something difficult or dangerous. What do you say for encouragement?

S7: Good luck.

T: Good. Now, Junsu and Minki, get together; Kyungsu and Jihi, get together; Nari and Sumi, get together. **Now, let's practice the idioms.** [2] **One of you will explain the idioms and the other finds them.** [3]

Reviewing Idioms

관용어의 복습

Expressions used

1) **What if I want you to wait on the phone?** : Means, what should I say if I stop the conversation for a moment or two on the phone; don't hang up the phone, just wait until I continue the conversation. 통화 중에 내가 잠시 대화를 중단하려면 무엇이라고 말해야 하는가라는 의미이다. 대화를 계속할 때까지 전화를 끊지 마라.

2) **Now, let's practice the idioms** : The students learned new idioms; now the teacher wants the students to practice using them in sentences. 학생들은 새로운 관용구를 배웠다. 이제 선생님은 학생들이 그것들을 문장 속에서 사용하는 것을 연습하기를 원한다.

3) **One of you will explain the idioms and the other find them** : These are directions for the students. One student will try to explain the meaning of an idiom, and the other try to guess which is the correct idiom. 이것은 지시문이다. 한 학생이 관용구의 의미를 설명하면, 다른 학생은 그에 맞는 올바른 관용구를 추측해야 한다.

Konglish vs English

구 분	Konglish	English
축약의 오류	볼펜(ball pen)	ball-point pen, plain pen
	노트(note)	notebook
	수정용 화이트(white)	white-out, correction pen
	사인(sign)	signature
	아파트(apart)	apartment
	캔음료(can)	canned beverage
	스킨(skin)	toner, aftershave
	원피스(one-piece)	(one-piece) dress
	나이트클럽(night club)	club, disco
	리모콘(remo-con)	remote control
	에어컨(air-con)	air conditioner
	프라이팬(fry pan)	(frying) pan, skillet
	광고방송(C.F.)	commercial, T.V. ad.
	(대학의)엠티(M.T.)	volunteering,
		community service,
		leadership training
	A/S	customer service
	핸드폰(Hand phone)	cell(ular) phone,
		cell, mobile phone
	디스카운트(D.C.)	discount, bargain
	하이힐(high heel)	high heels
		(pumps, stilettoes)
	카세트(cassette)	tape recorder, player
	테이프(tape)	audio (video), cassette tape

구 분	Konglish	English
의미의 오류	학생용 가방(sack)	backpack, school bag, knapsack
	호프	(beer) bar
	(차) 백미러(back mirror)	rear-view mirror
	핸들(handle)	steering wheel
	클랙슨(klaxon)	horn
	펑크(punk)	flat tire
	오토바이(auto-bi)	motor cycle, motor bike
	샤프 펜슬(sharp pencil)	mechanical pencil
	(차) 변속기(mission)	transmission
	스킨쉽(skinship)	cuddling, physical contact
	(컴퓨터) 노트북(notebook)	laptop
	호치키스(hotchkiss)	stapler
	컨닝(cunning)	cheating
	햄버거 세트(hamberger set)	hamburger combo
	개인별 부담(Dutch pay)	Dutch treat, go Dutch
	정장용 와이셔츠(Y-shirt)	Dress shirt
	콤비(Combi)	sport(s) jacket, blazer
	안개꽃(fog flowers)	Baby's breath
	스탠드(stand)	lamp
	프런트(front)	front desk, reception
	메니큐어(manicure)	nail polish
	큰아버지(big father)	father's older brother

Part 3

Which do you mean?; A woman without her man is nothing. [A woman, without her man, is nothing. OR A woman; without her, man is nothing.]
[Lynne Truss(2003), English Writer]

무슨 뜻이죠? 남편이 없는 여자가 별 볼 일 없는 건지, 여자 없이는 남자가 별 볼 일 없는 건지.

Grammar
문법

학습내용 ————

여기에는 원어민의 회화 수업 중 나올 수 있는 문법적인 사항에 대해 설명, 정리하였다. 어휘 자체의 문법적 특징, 어휘 간 용법의 차이, 문장에 관련된 문법, 대화문에 대한 문법의 오류 정정 등에 관한 학습 활동을 살펴보기로 한다. 원어민이 문법적인 사항을 설명한 것은 때로 모호한 면도 있으며, 문법 용어를 사용하여 형식적으로 알려주기보다는 일상적인 표현을 사용하여 자연스럽게 설명하려는 경향이 있다.

Family

가족

 가족에 대한 대화를 나누던 중 학생들의 잘못된 표현에 대한 오류를 수정하고 있다. 교과에서 다루지 않는 실제 상황에서 나올 수 있는 질문, 즉 개방된 질문(open question), 대상 관련 질문(referential question), 또는 발산성 질문(divergent question)에 대한 표현 능력을 향상시킬 필요가 있다는 것을 보여주고 있다.

T: Now, let's talk about our family!

S1: How many family do you want?

T: How many children do you want?

S1: When you marry?

T: When will you get married? I don't know. Appearance is not important. But she should be smart and intelligent.

S1: How about your family?

T: 'How about' is a desire.

S1: What do you think about your family. Do you like father or mother?

T: Who do you prefer, mother or father?

S2: Do you have penalties from your father?

T: Did you get punishment from father? I got a spanking or **I got grounded.** [1]

'To be grounded' means loss of freedom; no TV, no going outside. **You go to school and come back home, usually for one week or two weeks.** [2]

S5: What do your family want?

T: What's my family's expectation? What is expectation?

S5: Desire?

T: No. It has no condition. Now what's your parent's expectation for you to do?

 Penguin

Penguins are flightless birds, but they are very good swimmers and divers. They are also able to leap up out of the water onto ice or land at a height of up to two meters. The male penguin 'babysits' the single egg that a female penguin lays by rolling it up onto his feet to get it off the ice. He then keeps it warm for about two months until it hatches. (펭귄은 날지 못하는 새지만, 매우 빠른 수영 선수이며 다이빙 선수입니다. 그들은 2미터 높이의 얼음이나 육지에 뛰어오를 수 있습니다. 수컷 펭귄은 암컷 펭귄이 낳은 한 개의 알을 돌보면서, 발로 굴려 얼음을 털어냅니다. 그런 다음 그 알이 부화될 때까지 따뜻하게 약 2달간 지킵니다.)

Expressions used

1) **I got grounded** : This expression means that I got punished. 'Grounded' is a form of punishment whereby someone is not allowed to leave the house for a period of time. 이 말은 '나는 벌을 받았다'는 의미이다. 'Grounded'(외출 금지 시키다)는 처벌의 한 형태로, 일정 기간 집을 나가는 것을 금지당하는 것이다.

2) **You go to school and come back home usually for one week or two weeks** : The teacher is explaining the duration of her 'grounded' punishment. 선생님은 외출 금지 기간을 설명하고 있다.

World War II

 학생이 여성 해방 운동에 대한 수필을 읽는 도중에 'World War II'를 잘 못 읽자 선생님이 수정하고 있다.

S1: (While reading an essay about Women's Liberation) The basic causes in the United States can be traced to three events; the development of effective birth control methods, the invention of labor saving devices, and the advent of World War II [Second].

T: Uh uh. No, **you don't read World War II as World War Second.**[1] It should be World War Two. Got it?

Ss: Yeah. We got it!

T: And also, we don't use 'the' in front of World War Two. **It's just World War Two itself,**[2] like World War II[Two] began in···. However, if you say Second World War, then you should put 'the' in front of it. The Second World War began in···. Okay?

Expressions used

1) **you don't read World War II as World War second**: The teacher is explaining to the students that 'WWII' is not spoken as 'World War Second'.; it is spoken as 'World War Two'. 선생님이 WWII는 'World War Second'가 아닌 'World War Two'로 읽는다는 것을 학생들에게 설명하고 있다.

2) **It's just World War Two itself**: The teacher is explaining to the students that the definite article 'the' is not used with 'World War II[Two]' but the definite article is used with 'Second World War'. 선생님이 'World War II[Two]'에는 정관사 'the'가 사용되지 않고 'Second World War'에 는 정관사가 함께 사용된다는 점을 학생들에게 설명하고 있다.

Plural Form; Guy & Chalk

 보통 명사와 수량 명사의 복수형에 대한 설명을 하고 있다.

S: The guy is working in a corrupt law firm.

T: By the way, what's a guy?

Ss: Guy is a people!!

T: What? A guy is a people? It can't be a people. It should be….

S3: Person! A guy is a person.

T: Yeah! You're right. Guys are people and a guy is a person. Got it? Hmm. Now where is my chalk?

S1: Chalk? The chalks are over there. They're on the table.

T: Chalks? Actually, **we don't say chalks because chalk is an uncountable noun.**[1] Instead we say a piece of chalk, or pieces of chalk if you want it to be plural. Everyone got it?

Ss: Yes.

> **Tip** Agenda vs Data
> 'Agenda' is a noun with a Latin plural ending(the singular form is 'agendum'). However, it is used as a singular noun like 'data'.: What's on the agenda for today? ('Agenda'(의사 일정, 안건)는 라틴어의 복수형 어미를 가진 명사이다.(단수형은 'agendum'이다.) 그러나 'data'와 마찬가지로 단수로 사용된다.: '오늘 의사 일정이 무엇이니?')

Expressions used

1) **we don't say chalks because chalk is an uncountable noun**: We wouldn't say chalks because it's not countable(because you can't count it.) 분필은 셀 수 없기 때문에 'chalks'라고 하지 않는다.

Persons & People Unit 4

'인물들'과 '사람들'

 'person'의 복수형인 'persons'와 'people'의 화용적 차이에 대한 설명 이다.

T: Hello. **What brings you here?** [1]

S: Hi, John. I have a question. Is the word 'person' countable?

T: Yes, it is. Do you know its plural form?

S: Yes, it's 'people'. But can 'persons' be used as well? I found this sentence and I think it is wrong.

T: Let's see. 'This vehicle is authorized to carry twenty persons'. Grammatically it's correct. The word 'persons' is also the plural form of 'person'.

S: Then, **can I use 'people' and 'persons' in any sentence?** [2]

T: Not usually. The word 'persons' is usually used only in official or formal contexts. **In general conversation, the word 'people' is used.** [3] Do you understand the difference?

S: Yes, John. Thank you very much.

Expressions used

1) **What brings you here?** : Why are you here? Or, why are you visiting? 웬일로 왔니?

2) **can I use 'people' and 'persons' in any sentence?** : The student is asking if these words are interchangeable.
학생이 이 두 개의 단어가 서로 교체될 수 있는지 묻고 있다.

3) **In general conversation, the word 'people' is used** : The word 'people' is used in less formal situations.
일상적인 경우에는 'people'이 사용된다.

Didn't & Couldn't

Didn't와 Couldn't

 단순 부정의 의미를 가진 'didn't'와 금지의 뜻을 가진 'couldn't'의 의미 차이를 분명히 할 것을 요구하고 있다.

T: Good morning!

Ss: Good morning!

T: How are you guys feeling today?

S1: Not very well.

T: Really? **How come?**[1]

S2: Our class had the lowest score and we had to study for the TEPS test.

S1: So we didn't go out for the weekend.

T: **Didn't or couldn't?**[2]

S1: Um, couldn't.

T: Ah··· That's too bad.

Tip Contractions

Words like 'I've', 'won't', and 'shouldn't' are called contractions. These shorter forms (for 'I have', 'I will not', and 'I should not') use an apostrophe to show where a letter has been taken out. ('I've', 'won't', and 'shouldn't'와 같은 단어를 단축형[축약형]이라 부른다. 이런 단축 형태는 문자가 생략된 곳을 나타내기 위해서 아포스트로피를 붙인다.)

Expressions used

1) **How come?** : Why? What happened? 왜? 무슨 일이니?

2) **Didn't or couldn't?** : You didn't go out or you couldn't go out? 외출하지 않았니? 못했니?

전치사에 대한 연습 문제를 통하여, 학생들이 가장 많이 틀리는 전치사 'in'과 'on'의 용법 차이에 대해 설명하고 있다.

T: Today we will go over the proper usages of prepositions. On the sheet of paper that I'm handing out, there are several questions regarding prepositions. You have 20 minutes to complete them.

Example Questions

1. **Mary is going (　) buy a new car.**
2. **John is making use (　) his authority.**
3. **Sam is going to fishing (　) the weekend.**
4. **Please bring your homework (　) time.**
5. **My mother is (　) the mall.**

(After 3 min)

T: I noticed that most of you got number 4 wrong. Who can tell me the correct answer?

S1: It is the preposition, 'in'. It should read, "Please bring your homework in time."

T: Incorrect! I will explain to you what the correct answer is and why. The correct answer is 'on'. The answer should be, 'Please bring your homework on time'. The answer you have given me, 'in', is a preposition you use when talking about a non-specific time. Like the sentence 'in the year 2005'. A year is a long term and broad extent of time. It can be a long term. 'On' is a preposition used when talking about a specific time. **A specific date, holidays are included in the usage of 'on'.**[1] For example, 'I will try to come on Monday'. Do you get it now?

Ss: Yes. We understand!

Tip 'Upon' and 'On'

'Upon' and 'On' are synonymous and interchangeable.: He threw himself upon the bed. She walked on a tightrope. 'Upon' is slightly more formal, and in speaking 'on' is usually preferred. ('Upon'과 'On'은 동의어로 대체할 수 있습니다.: 그는 침대에 몸을 던졌다. 그녀는 줄 위에서 걸었다. 'Upon'은 다소 공식적이며, 구어에서는 대개 'On'을 선호합니다.)

Expressions used

1) **A specific date, holidays are included in the usage of 'on'**: The teacher is explaining to the students that we use the preposition 'on' when we are talking about dates. For example: 'On January 25'. Holidays are specific dates, so 'on' is used. For example: 'On Christmas Day'. 선생님은 날짜에 대해 말할 때에는 전치사 'on'을 사용한다고 학생들에게 설명하고 있다. 예를 들면 'On January 25.' 휴일은 특별한 날이다. 그래서 'on'이 사용된다. 예를 들면, 'On Christmas Day'.

[Cartoon] About Watches

If-clause

다음은 'if' 절에 대한 두 가지 교수 방법이다. 두 가지 교수법이 뚜렷이 대비되는 의미 있는 자료로 교수 평가 과정에서 저자가 직접 참관한 자료이다. 전자는 영문학을 전공한 원어민 선생님의 수업으로, 모국어 학습과 같이 일상적인 담화를 통해 자연스럽게 언어를 습득하는 것을 중시하는 직접 교수법(direct method)에서 발전한 의사 소통 방법(Communicative teaching method)에 가깝다. 반면 후자는 영어 교육학을 전공한 원어민 선생님의 수업으로 문법 번역식 교수법(grammar translation method)에서 발전한 전통적인 교수법(Traditional teaching method)에 가까운 학습 방법이다. 그 차이를 살펴보면 교수법의 개발에 도움이 될 것이다.

A. If (with communicative teaching method)

일상적인 대화를 통해 문법 용어를 사용하지 않고 'if' 조건절의 용법을 설명하고 있다.

T: Did you ever buy a Lotto ticket?

S1: No.

T: Never?

S1: Never.

T: But it's a lot of money.

S2: I bought it.

T: Yeah. Well, what are you thinking when you buy the ticket?

S2: I'll buy a BMW.

S3: Go abroad.

S4: Save.

T: Save? Are you sure?

S5: I'll help poor people, and handicapped people.

S6: I'll buy some cars. (He pronounces 's' as [s], not [z])

T: Not cars. Carzzz!! Alright! While you have those tickets, you are thinking, "Maybe, maybe··· But you don't say, "When I win Lotto, I'll buy some cars". What do we say?

Ss: (No answer)

T: We don't say 'when' when we aren't 100% sure. 'When' means it's going to happen 100% certainly. To win the Lotto is not 100% certain. When you are old, you will retire. It is 100% certain. But you may not win the Lotto. Therefore we shouldn't say 'when' when we talk about Lotto. We should say···.

(Teacher waits until the correct answer comes.)

S3: While.

T: Nope.

S4: If?

T: Yes. Absolutely. **That little word!** [1] Here are examples. If I win Lotto I might retire. If I win Lotto I could give the money to the poor. If I win Lotto I might be able to buy a house. 'If' is a conditional word. It's not 100%, it's only possibility. Then we have a consequence. A consequence means the results of something; I would, I could, I should. Those are consequences….

Now repeat, "If I win Lotto I would buy a car".

Ss: If I win Lotto I would buy a car.

T: **How about in reverse?** [2] Reverse the parts of the sentence. Be creative.

Ss: I would buy a car if I win Lotto.

T: Excellent. See. You can reverse. It doesn't matter. Everybody got it?

Ss: Yeah.

T: Alright! **Pretty easy stuff!** [3] Talk about yourself using 'if'.

(He asks each student.)

S: ….

T: Now do you know why this is important?

S: Umm…

T: Because we do it all the time whenever we make a decision. When you came to the university you used 'if'; "If I go to the teachers college I might get a stable job." Something like this.

S: Yes.

T: So it's very important.

If-clause

if절

Expressions used

1) **That little word!** : Referring to the importance of such a little word like 'if' and its meaning in sentences. 문장에서 'if'와 같은 작은 단어의 중요성과 그 의미를 언급하고 있다.

2) **How about in reverse?** : How about switching the order. The teacher is asking the students to reverse the order of the clauses. 선생님은 절의 순서를 바꿔보면 어떻겠느냐고 학생에게 묻고 있다.
Ex : Dependent clause + independent : If I won the Lotto I would buy a sports car.
Independent clause + dependent : I would buy a sports car if I won the Lotto.

3) **Pretty easy stuff!** : This material we are learning is not difficult. 우리가 배우는 이 내용은 어렵지 않다.

reference

Nina Spada(2007)에서 보면, 의사소통적 언어 교수법(communicative language teaching : CLT)에는 '상호 활동을 통한 자유로운 의사 소통이 외국어 학습에 효과적이다'는 전제 하에 다음 5가지 특징을 들고 있다.

1) focus on meaning(의미 중점)
2) little explicit feedback on learner error(최소한의 수정)
3) learner-centered teaching(학습자 중심 교육)
4) listening and speaking practice(듣기 및 말하기 연습)
5) avoidance of the learner's L1(모국어 사용 금지)

B. If (with traditional teaching method)

전통적인 판서를 이용한 설명 방법으로 'if'의 용법을 가르치고 있다. 문법 설명을 마친 뒤에 그룹별로 예문을 만들고, 다음으로 각 그룹의 개개인이 자신이 만든 예문을 읽게 한 뒤, 문법적 오류를 수정하고 있다.

T: Good morning.

S: Good morning. sir.

T: Take a look at the board. Can I get the groups' attention?

(Before class the students are already divided into 2 groups [8 people in each group]. Each group has one captain and his/her members.)

Look at the board. Repeat after me.

(On the board the following is already written before class.)

▶Topic : Conditional clauses with 'if' clauses

They describes possible situations and consequences.

Conditional sentences:

Statements and questions about something that could possibly happen provided a certain condition exists or a certain event occurs.

Situation: Event

Consequences: Result

If I learn English, I might become a translator.

If he quits school, he won't be able to graduate.

If you study hard, you'll learn a lot more.

....

T: (teacher explains simply.)

Situation, 'If I learn English', Result, 'I might become a translator'.

Situation, 'If he quits school', Result, 'he won't be able to graduate'.

Situation, 'If you study hard', Result, 'you'll learn a lot more'.

T: Now, open your books to page 57. Match A with B.

(In the textbook, New Interchange Book2)

T: Chulsu A, Nami B. Number 1.

Chulsu: If you eat less sugar,

If-clause

Q: Match the clauses in column A with the information from column B.

A	B
1. If you eat less sugar,	a. you may feel more relaxed.
2. If you walk to work everyday,	b. you might feel healthier.
3. If you don't get enough sleep,	c. you won't be able to stay awake in class.
4. If you own a pet,	d. you'll have less money to spend on yourself.
5. If you don't get married,	e. you won't be able to stay awake in class.

Nami: you may feel healthier.

T: Good job. Now use part A and write B. Use your own ideas. I want you to think with your own idea. Now, take 3 minutes. Write your own ideas. I'll look at your grammar.

(teacher is looking around while students are making up sentences.)

(After a moment)

T: (The captain of group A is Yongsu.)

Have you finished, Youngsu?

Youngsu: Yes.

T: Read your sentence.

Youngsu: If you are unmarried, you'll save much money.

T: If you remain single, you'll save a lot of money.

Youngsu: If you remain single, you'll save a lot of money.

T: Good job! Good! Now, Sukhi, how about your answer?

(Sukhi is the captain of group B.)

Sukhi: If you don't sleep at night, we can't go out on weekend.

T: **Be careful of your grammar.**[1] We won't be able to go out on the weekend. Do you have any questions? Now, everyone, use part A and write B on your own.

Tip Drank vs Drunk

Be careful to use 'drank' and 'drunk'. 'Drank' is the past tense of 'drink'.: He drank the whole can. 'Drunk' is the past participle and goes with 'have' or 'be'.: I've drunk my milk. A person who is drunk has had too much alcohol. ('drank'와 'drunk'의 사용에 유의하라. 'drank'는 'drunk'의 과거시제이다.: 그는 캔을 통째로 마셨다. 'drunk'는 과거분사로 'have' 또는 'be'와 함께 사용된다.: 나는 우유를 마셨다. 취한 사람은 술을 너무 많이 마셨다.)

Expressions used

1) **Be careful of your grammar**: Watch your grammar.
문법에 유의하세요.

Tense

 동사의 시제와 형용사의 활용형에 대한 설명이다. 마지막에 선생님의 지시에 대해 학생이 단어를 사용하지 않고 사건을 이야기하고 있어 이를 정정해 주고 있다.

A. Past tense and past participle

T: What is the past tense and the past participle of the word, 'burn'?

S1: Burned, and burneded!

T: Almost correct, but you got the past participle wrong.[1] Who else would like to try?

S2: Burned and burnt!

T: Correct! Would you also give me a sentence using the past participle of the word, 'burn'?

S2: Tony went to the burnt house, which he once lived in.

T: Excellent! In your final exams, **you will be given questions that regard the past tense and past participle of a word.**[2] Be prepared! Who can tell me the noun form of the word, 'sick'?

S3: I think that it is sicking.

T: Incorrect! Let me give you a hint. The noun form of the word 'ill' is illness.

S3: It is sickness!

T: Correct! **Can you also put that in a sentence using the noun form?**[3]

S4: Okay. I will try! I had traffic accident, so I went to hospi-

Tense

tal 2 weeks.

T: You left out the article! Never forget to use articles to achieve proper usage of English. The sentence should have been "I had a traffic accident, so I went to the hospital for 2 weeks".

Expressions used

1) **Almost correct, but you got the past participle wrong** : The teacher is telling the student that his/her answer was almost correct. The only part the student got wrong was his/her use of the past participle. 선생님이 학생에게 답이 거의 정확하다고 말하고 있다. 학생이 틀린 부분은 과거완료의 사용이다.

2) **you will be given questions that regard the past tense and past participle of a word** : The teacher is telling the students what will be on the test : that they should be prepared to know both the past tense and past participle forms of the verbs. 선생님은 학생들에게 무엇이 시험에 출제될 것인지를 말하고 있다.: 학생들은 동사의 과거시제와 과거완료의 형식을 알아 두어야 한다고 말하고 있다.

3) **Can you also put that in a sentence using the noun form?** : The teacher is asking the student to use the adjective 'sick' as the noun 'sickness' in a sentence. 선생님은 학생에게 문장에서 형용사 'sick' 을 명사 'sickness'로 사용할 것을 요구하고 있다.
   ▶ 다음에 이어지는 학생의 대답은 명사 'sickness'가 아닌 실제 병원에 입원한 사례를 예로 들었지만 선생님은 그대로 계속 진행하고 있다.

B. past tense and present perfect sentences

선생님이 학생들에게 '과거' 시제와 '현재완료' 시제를 이용하여 각
각 2개의 문장을 만들 것을 지시한 뒤, 둘러 보면서 개개인의 문장의
틀린 점을 지적하고 있다.

....

T: OK. Today we are going to begin our class with an
activity! I want you to open your books. I want you to
make 2 past tense and present perfect sentences each. 2
each. Alright? Let's go! Take charge!

Ss: Take charge!

T: (In a few minutes) Insu, how are you? Good. Still thinking?
(Looking at Insu's writing) 'Did you take a shower?' That
means 'did you clean your body?' OK. How do you spell
squash?

Insu: S-Q-U-A-C-H-Y.

T: Nope! That will be 'squachy'!! Hehehe.

Ss: Hahaha.

T: James! How are you doing? 'How do you smell?' What do
you mean? But that is a present tense question. We want
past tense or present perfect.

You can ask that question, but you need to make 2 past
tense and present perfect sentences.

James: OK.

T: Uh-oh. What is the past participle of 'go'?

S: Um…

T: Gone!!

S: Ah ha.

T: How about the past participle of 'make'?

S: Make, made, made.

T: Good.

S: Gerry, I don't know how to spell Niagara Falls.

T: Don't worry about the spelling. N.I.A.G.A.R.A.F.A.L.L.S.
Alright. Jason, are you finished with the question?

Jason: How do you spell Lotte World?

T: You don't know how to spell Lotte World? Lotte and
World as a universe.

Jason: OK. I get it.

T: OK. Everyone finished with your discussions? Then start
with your conversations. **Captain Roh, what's going on?**[1]
You and you and you have to start a conversation.
(Students start their discussion.)

S: Is sushi raw fish?

T: Yes, sushi is raw fish. Have you ever tried squash? It's a very good sport.

S: Um, no.

T: Then have you ever tried pizza?

Ss: Yes!

S: Have you ever tried drugs?

T: What kind of drugs?

S: Marijuana, cocaine.

T: Nope⋯ never tried those before. Good discussion! **I want a lot of noise here.** [2] Did you see Mike Tyson on television yesterday?

Ss: No. What happened?

T: Mike Tyson lost. He was winning but he didn't come out of his corner. I don't know why, but he was winning.

Expressions used

1) **Captain Roh, what's going on?** : Captain Roh is a student's nickname. The teacher is asking him/her what is the matter or what is wrong. 노 반장은 학생의 별명이다. 선생님은 무엇이 문제인지 묻고 있다.

2) **I want a lot of noise here** : The teacher is saying he wants a lot of active participation by the students during the discussion. 선생님은 학생들이 토의에 활발하게 참석할 것을 원한다고 말하고 있다.

Dialogue Correction

대화 수정

먼저 유인물에 나타난 두 개의 대화, 미팅 준비와 미팅을 읽고 학생들과 함께 한 문장씩 오류를 확인하고 수정하는 활동이다. 먼저 편의상 대화문 다음에 수정된 정답을 표시하였다. 정답 다음에는 〈대화 내용〉에서 구체적으로 학생이 읽고 선생님이 수정하는 과정을 대화체로 기록하였으므로 실제 영어로 오류 정정 수업을 진행하는 데 많은 도움이 될 것이다.

〈유인물〉

DIRECTIONS

Read the following dialogues and correct all of the mistakes. The situation is; Mike and Steven are friends. Mike set up a blind date for Steven and Jennifer. The first dialogue is between Mike and Steven(friends) and the next dialogue is between Steven and Jennifer(first date). There are a total of 47 mistakes(17 in the first dialogue and 30 in the second dialogue).

··

〈문제1〉

[TALK]

Mike: Steven, are you ready for your meeting tonight?

Steven: Actually, I feel like nervous. Do you mind if I ask you a question?

Mike: Yes, what is it?

Steven: How does she look like?

Mike: Well, she's very cute. She has long hair and big eyes. She looks like really beautiful.

Steven: You know, the last time I had a meeting, it was

terrible. Don't you remember?

Mike: Yes, I don't remember. I'm so sorry to hear that.

Steven: That's okay. I just wish tonight is funny, you know? I worked so hardly to make everything perfect. I cut my hair and I bought these new pant. One last thing, can you borrow me your car?

Mike: Sorry, but I have to go my home soon. My mother needs the car.

Steven: PLEASE. Until now, I have never had a good first date. You know, I really want to make a girlfriend. I haven't made a girlfriend since 3 years!

Mike: Okay, I will tell to my mother that you really need the car. Don't worry. Good luck!

....

(정답1)

Mike: Steven, are you ready for your <u>meeting</u> tonight?
<small>'date', 'blind date'</small>

Steven: Actually, I feel <u>like</u> nervous. Do you mind if I ask
<small>'like'삭제</small>
you a question?

Mike: Yes, what is it?

Steven: How does she look like?
'What'

Mike: Well, she's very cute. She has long hair and big eyes.
really beautiful

She looks like really beautiful.
'like'삭제

Steven: You know, the last time I had a meeting, it was
a date

terrible. Don't you remember?

Mike: Yes, I don't remember. I'm so sorry to hear that.
'No, I don't' 또는 'Yes, I do.'

Steven: That's okay. I just wish tonight is funny, you know?
'hope'   'fun'

I worked so hardly to make everything perfect. I cut my
'hard'   'got a hair-cut'

hair and I bought these new pant. One last thing, can you
'pants'

borrow me your car?
'lend'

Mike: Sorry, but I have to go my home soon. My mother
'my'삭제

needs the car.

Steven: PLEASE. Until now, I have never had a good first

date. You know, I really want to make a girlfriend. I haven't
'have' 또는 'get'

made a girlfriend since 3 years!
'had'   'in' 또는 'for'

Mike: Okay, I will tell to my mother that you really need the
'to'삭제

car. Don't worry. Good luck!

(문제2)

[AT THE DATE]

Steven: Hello, I'm Steven. Nice to see you.

Jennifer: Nice to see you, too. I'm Jennifer. I'm from New York. Where are you come from?

Steven: I'm from Boston. What do you do? I'm a student at Naval Academy.

Jennifer: I'm a student too but I don't like studying.

Steven: Me too! I'm so boring everyday doing homework and taking tests.

Jennifer: Recently, I'm also so hard to study. I think almost students are the same.

Steven: I understand. When will you graduate university?

Jennifer: Two years later. How about you?

Steven: After one year. How do you think about your university?

Jennifer: So-so. What are you doing while vacation?

Steven: I'm not sure yet, but I wish to trip to the China while vacation.

Jennifer: Oh, I envy you! When I was high school, I went to there.

Steven: Really? What are you doing during vacation?

Jennifer: I just want to take a rest.

Steven: What do you do in your free time?

Jennifer: I like to see the movie and take a picture. How about you?

Steven: I like to read a book, listen music and sing a song.

Jennifer: You like to sing a song? Well, let's sing a song together. Today is my birthday!

Steven: Congratulations!!!

....

(정답2)

Steven: Hello, I'm Steven. Nice to see you.
_{'to meet you' 또는 'meeting you'}

Jennifer: Nice to see you, too. I'm Jennifer. I'm from New
_{meet}
York. Where are you come from?
_{삭제}

Steven: I'm from Boston. What do you do? I'm a student at

Naval Academy.
_{'the Naval Academy'}

Jennifer: I'm a student too but I don't like studying.

Steven: Me too! I'm so <u>boring</u> everyday doing homework
'bored'
and taking tests.

Jennifer: Recently, <u>I'm also so hard to study</u>. I think <u>almost</u>
'I've been studying so hard'   'almost all'
students are the same.
'are doing'

Steven: I <u>understand</u>. When will you <u>graduate</u> university?
'see'   'graduate from'

Jennifer: Two years <u>later</u>. How about you?
'from now'

Steven: After one year. <u>How</u> do you think about your uni-
'What'
versity?

Jennifer: <u>So-so</u>. What are you doing <u>while</u> vacation?
'It's okay'   'for', 'on', 'during'

Steven: I'm not sure yet, but I wish to <u>trip</u> to <u>the China</u> <u>while</u>
'take a trip'   'China'   'on'
vacation.

Jennifer: <u>Oh, I envy you!</u> When I was <u>high</u> school, I went <u>to</u>
'I'm so envious/jealous'   'in high'   삭제
there.

Steven: Really? <u>What are you doing during vacation?</u>
'What are you goint to do for your vacation?'

Jennifer: <u>I just want to take a rest.</u>
'I just want to take it easy/ to get some rest.'

Steven: What do you do in your free time?

Dialogue Correction 대화 수정

Jennifer: I like to see the movie and take a picture. How

'movies' 'pictures'
about you?

Steven: I like to read a book, listen music and sing a song.

'books' 'listen to' 'songs'
Jennifer: You like to sing a song? Well, let's sing a song

'songs' 'some songs'
together. Today is my birthday!

Steven: Congratulations!!

'Happy birthday!/ Really? Oh.'

대화 내용

다음은 앞의 두 대화 [Talk]와 [At The Date]를 수정하는 과정을 수록
하였다. 먼저 학생들이 차례로 원문을 읽게 하고, 선생님이 읽은 문
장의 오류를 수정하는 방식으로 담화가 진행되고 있다. 수정 과정에
서 사용된 원어민의 표현을 익혀두면 영어를 이용한 오류 수정 활동
에 도움이 될 것이다.

....

(After reading the above dialogue)

T: That's my mistake. There are actually 48 mistakes. In the first dialogue, 18 mistakes. In the second, 30 mistakes. You will have about 20 minutes for this quiz.

S: (while correcting the errors in the dialogue) What is a blind date?

T: It's a date with somebody that we have never met before. (In 20 mins) Now, have you finished?

Ss: No.

T: Okay. One more minute···. Hey, pencils down. And we are going to check the answers. Change the papers. Have the red pencils in the middle.

S: (A student sneezes.)

T: What do you say when somebody sneezes?

S: God bless you.

T: God bless you or God bless. Why do we say that?

S: ….

T: Because when we sneeze, our breath stops for a moment…. Now, we'll begin with Mr. Kim. And we'll go around.

(Now the students read the dialogue and the teacher starts to correct the dialogue.)

[TALK]

Mr. Kim: Steven, are you ready for your date tonight?

T: Date or blind date… fine.

S2: Actually, I feel like nervous. Do you mind if I ask you a question?

T: There is just one mistake here. I feel nervous.

S3: Yes, what is it?

S4: How does she look like?

T: What does she look like? Not, how does she look like.

S5: Well, she's very cute. She has long hair and big eyes. She looks like really beautiful.

T: Cute. She looks really beautiful.

S6: You know, the last time I had a meeting, it was terrible. Don't you remember?

T: ….

S7: Yes, I don't remember. I'm so sorry to hear that.

T: No, I don't or yes, I do. Either one is OK.

S8: That's okay. I just wish tonight is funny, you know?

T: Not funny, fun. **I just hope tonight is fun.** [1] Keep going.

S8: I worked so hardly to make everything perfect. I cut my hair and I bought these new pant. One last thing, can you borrow me your car?

T: First, **I worked so hard to make everything perfect.** Second, **I got a hair-cut and these new pants.** Last sentence, **lend, not borrow.**

S9: Sorry, but I have to go my home soon. My mother needs the car.

T: **I have to go home, not my home.**

S10: PLEASE. Until now, I have never had a good first date. You know, I really want to make a girlfriend. I haven't made a girlfriend since 3 years!

T: I really want to have a girlfriend. I haven't had a girlfriend. **In 3 years or for 3 years. Either one is OK.**

S11: Okay, I will tell to my mother that you really need the car. Don't worry. Good luck!

T: I will tell my mother. Any question on dialogue 1? Tell me

Dialogue Correction 대화 수정

the number correct, not incorrect. Let's start dialogue two.

....

[AT THE DATE]

T: Now, second dialogue. Let's begin with Steven.

S2: Hello, I'm Steven. Nice to see you.

T: **When you meet for the first time, nice to meet you.**
Second, third, fourth, 100th time··· nice to see you.

S3: Nice to see you too. I'm Jennifer. I'm from New York.
Where are you come from?

T: Where do you come from or where are you from. **'Where
are you from?' is more common.**

S4: I'm from Boston. What do you do? I'm a student at Naval
Academy.

T: **At the Naval Academy.**

S5: I'm a student too but I don't like studying.

T: That's OK.

S6: Me too! I'm so boring everyday doing homework and
taking tests.

T: **Bored, not boring.**

S7: Recently, I'm also so hard to study. I think almost all
students are the same.

T: First sentence. Recently I've been studying hard. Second, almost all students are doing the same. **Almost all is plural. Almost every is singular.**

S8: I understand. When will you graduate university?

T: **'I understand' is too formal. 'I see' is more common like delicious is formal and good is informal.** Not graduate university but graduate from your university. Or when are you going to graduate from the university?

S9: Two years later. How about you?

T: **'Later' is OK, but 'Two years from now' is more common.**

S10: After one year. How do you think about your university?

T: What do you think?

S11: So-so. What are you doing while vacation?

T: Two mistakes are here. **What happens to so-so?**

S: (silent)

T: Just erase. **We don't say so-so. We say it's OK.** What are you going to do on vacation, or for or during your vacation. **For is more common than during.**

S2: I'm not sure yet, but I wish to trip to the China while vacation.

T: 'I'm not sure yet' is OK. But I want to go to China on vacation.

S3: Oh, I envy you! When I was high school, I went to there.

T: **'I envy you', that's correct but 'I'm so jealous or envious' is better.** I was in high school or I was a high school student. Not, 'I went to there' but I went there, too.

S4: Really? What are you doing during vacation?

T: What are you going to do for your vacation or on your vacation?

S5: I just want to take a rest.

T: 'Take a rest'. No. I hate that. **I just want to get some rest.**

S: Why?

T: Don't say 'Why'. You should say 'Why is that? or could you tell me the reason?'. **'Take a rest' is OK but we don't use it. We usually use 'get'.** So, we say 'We want to get some rest or to take a nap'.

S6: What do you do in your free time?

T: **No mistakes here.**

S7: I like to see the movie and take a picture. How about you?

T: Mistake number 1, watch movies. Mistake number 2, take pictures.

S8: I like to read a book, listen music and sing a song.

T: 'Read' or 'read books' are OK. Listen to music and sing. We don't need 'a song'. **When we sing, we know it's a song.**

S9: You like to sing a song? Well, let's sing a song together. Today is my birthday!

T: That's O.K.

S10: Congratulations!!

T: Happy birthday! **Congratulations, it means good news. Birthday is not always happy especially when you are old.** You can say congratulations when she got a promotion or passed her examinations.

T: Count the number correct. Say the total number correct. Mr. Choi, what happened to you?

Mr. Choi: My goal for this quiz is above 30. I know this material is not easy.

T: Keep practicing and practicing. Did everyone get perfect? Perfect scores? Now, please give this back to me.

Tip Husband

'Husband' comes from an Old Norse word meaning 'master of a household'. It was generally applied to all men who were masters of a household whether married or single.
('남편'은 '가정의 주인'이라는 의미를 가진 고대 아이슬란드 어에서 유래되었다. 그것은 미혼이건 기혼이건 가정의 주인인 모든 남자에게 적용되었다.)

Cartoon

[Cartoon] Two Friends

Passive Voice

 수동태를 만드는 방법에 대한 설명이다. 먼저 칠판에 쓰인 내용을 모두 따라 읽게 한 뒤에 수동태를 이용한 문장을 만들라고 지시하고 있다.

(The following is written on the board)

The book was written(p.p.) **by him.**

The food will be eaten(p.p.) **by me.** (passive)

Object + be + pp + by + subject

e.g. **English is used by many people.**

....

T: What is an example of a passive voice using the present tense? [1]

Ss: ….

T: Let's think of language as an example. If we think about the language that a country uses?

S1: English is used by many people.

T: Correct, but we don't have to always use 'by', so we can just say, 'English is used in America'.

Why do we use the passive voice?

S2: To express the subject.

T: Yes. **There is one important thing I'm trying to tell you.** [2] You shouldn't use the passive voice if possible. In Korea, you learn passive voice, and they are on the exams, but you should not use it if you don't have to.

S3: Because Koreans don't use passive?

Passive Voice

T: Also we don't use it very often, but you should still know about it.

Tip Avoid using 'Quite'

Be careful how you use 'quite' because this little word can mean 'very' or 'sort of'. 'This cake is quite good' could mean fairly good but not very good. But there is no doubt about 'This cake is quite excellent'. So it might be quite a good idea to avoid using 'quite', if it's going to cause offence. ('Quite'는 '매우' 또는 '다소' 두 의미가 있으므로 사용할 때 주의하세요. 'This cake is quite good'은 다소 좋지만 매우 좋지는 않다는 의미일 수 있습니다. 그러나 '이 케이크는 매우 뛰어나다.'는 분명합니다. 따라서 불쾌할 수도 있는 경우에는 'quite'를 사용하는 것을 피하는 것이 좋은 생각입니다.)

Expressions used

1) **What is an example of a passive voice using the present ten-se?** : The teacher is simply asking the students to give an example of the grammar. 선생님이 학생들에게 문법에 대한 예시를 제시하라고 요청하고 있다.

2) **There is one important thing I'm trying to tell you** : The teacher is emphasizing an important point. 선생님은 중요한 점을 강조하고 있다.

Relative Pronoun

관계대명사

 관계대명사의 용법에 대한 설명이다. 먼저 'relative'의 의미를 물은 다음 관계대명사의 종류를 설명한 뒤, 교과서의 예문을 관계대명사를 이용하여 결합할 것을 지시하고 있다.

T: We're going to study relative clauses. Do you know what a relative is? Anyone?

S1: To express 'connection'.

T: Yeah. **It simply means 'connection'.**[1] Then what about relative pronouns? Any guess?

Ss: (silent)

T: A relative pronoun is a pronoun that connects sentences. There are three main relative pronouns which are who, which and that.

Who and that can be used to tell something about a person or people.

Which and that are used to describe things. So, when you are confused with the usage of who or which, you could use that in any place.

But! However, I don't want you guys to use 'that' on the final exams because I want to see how well you understood about the relative clauses. Alright?

Ss: Okay. We got it!

T: For example, now try to combine the sentences written in the book. 'It's about a guy. He joins a corrupt law firm.' What does 'corrupt' mean in this sentence?

S2: Dishonest?

T: Yeah. Dishonest, which is very bad.

Now, any volunteer to read the sentence with a relative clause?

Expressions used

1) **It simply means connection:** The teacher is telling the students that the word 'relative' can be similar to the word 'connection'. If something is related to something else, there is a connection.
선생님은 학생들에게 단어 'relative'는 단어 'connection'과 유시히디고 말하고 있다. 만약에 어떤 것이 다른 것과 관련되어 있으면 연관이 있는 것이다.

Part 4

My dear friend, clear your mind of cant. You may talk as other people do; you may say to a man, "Sir, I am your most humble servant." You are not his most humble servant⋯. You tell a man, "I am sorry you had such bad weather the last day of your journey, and were so much wet." You don't care six-pence whether he was wet or dry. You may talk in this manner; it is a mode of talking in Society; but don't think foolishly.'
[James Boswell(1740~1795), Scotch Author]

친구야. 너의 마음에서 위선을 지워라. 너는 남들처럼 말하는구나.: 너는 어떤 남자에게 "선생님, 기꺼이 봉사하겠습니다." 라고 말하지만 너는 그의 가장 비천한 하인이 아니다. ⋯ 또 어떤 남자에게 "오는 도중 마지막에 날씨가 안 좋아 흠뻑 젖었군요."라고 말한다. 너는 그가 젖었건 말랐건 한 푼도 신경을 쓰지 않는다. 너는 이런 식으로 말하는구나.: 그것은 사회에서 말하는 방식이다.: 그렇지만 바보 같이 생각하지는 말아라.

Speaking & Presentation
말하기와 발표

학습내용 ─────
여기에서는 먼저 공손한 언어 표현을 위한 유의 사항을 살펴본다. 다음으로 주어진 어휘 또는 일상적인 소재를 이용한 자유로운 대화, 그리고 지시에 따라 문장 만들기 및 문제 해결, 마지막으로 주제별 발표 및 토론의 기준, 주제별 토론 또는 발표의 순서로 정리하였다.

 수업 중에 학생들이 흔히 사용하는 세 가지 불손한 표현 'Yeah', 'Hey', 'What'의 의미와 이를 대체할 수 있는 표현에 대한 설명이다.

T: What does 'polite' mean?

S1: Like.

S2: Custom.

T: Kind of having a good attitude⋯ good manners, we say polite. How do you spell 'polite'?

Ss: P.O.L.I.T.E.

T: Yes, polite. **What is the opposite of polite?** [1] Rude or⋯?

S3: Manner.

T: Not manner⋯ it's Konglish.

S4: Im⋯

T: Sorry, I didn't hear you.

S4: Inpolite.

T: Impolite.

S4: Inpolite.

T: Im. Im-polite.

Ss: Impolite.

T: Later in the semester, we are going to have a lesson about being polite and impolite, because much of your English right now is sometimes impolite.

S2: Our English?

S1: Sometimes bad words?

T: I know that you are very, very polite people, but sometimes

Impolite Expressions 불손한 표현

you don't realize that you are being a little bit rude.

Again I'll talk more about it later, but I'll tell you four things first. So listen carefully. When I was taking attendance, many of you said 'yeah'. It is very impolite.

S3: What do we have to say?

T: You should say 'yes' instead of 'yeah'.

S2: Does it have other meaning in English?

T: If you say 'yeah' it's OK with your friends. But with your teachers or seniors or officers it's very rude. So that's number 1.

Ss: Yes, sir!

T: Ma'am, not sir.

Ss: Yes, ma'am!

T: Next, a lot of the students like to use 'hey' when calling someone. It's okay, you're friends, but it's very impolite for officers or teachers or other seniors. I'd say to Minho, 'Hey, Minho', but I wouldn't say, 'Hey, 교장'. What would I say?

S4: Hello.

T: Okay, what else? What's better than hello?

S2: Excuse me.

T: Yes.

T: For number 3, what students say a lot is, 'What'.

S5: (우리말로) 뭐? 맞지?

Ss: Haha….

T: 'I beg your pardon?', 'Excuse me?', 'I'm sorry, I didn't hear you'. All of these are OK but please don't say 'What?'

S1: Okay.

T: For number 4, **sometimes students like to use bad words.** [2] Please don't use bad words in class. Sometimes students don't know if it's good or bad, so I will tell you if it's a bad word. Please don't use them after I tell you.

Ss: Yes, ma'am!

T: I also have a couple of things that I want to tell you. I told you to bring a notebook this class last time.

When you're studying English, these are four questions that are very, very common. [3] When students ask questions, they ask in a wrong way, so keep note.

(Nina writes on the whiteboard.)

When you ask a spelling, this is the way to ask; 'How do you spell _____'.

If you don't know what a word means, this is how to ask; 'What does _____ mean?'

T: Is everyone writing this down?

Ss: Yes.

T: Number three, if you don't know the pronunciation, if you don't know how to say something you can say; 'How do you pronounce/say this word _____ ?'
If there is a word in Korean that you want to say in English or the other way, this is how to ask; 'How do you say _____ in English/Korean?' Please make sure you know all of these questions. OK?

Ss: Yes!

Expressions used

1) **What is the opposite of polite?**: The teacher is asking for an antonym of 'polite'. 선생님이 'polite'의 반의어를 묻고 있다.

2) **sometimes students like to use bad words**: Sometimes students like to use swear words or words that have very negative or disrespectful meanings. 때때로 학생들은 욕설이나 부정적 또는 불손한 의미를 지닌 말을 즐겨 사용한다.

3) **When you're studying English, these are four questions that are very, very common**: The teacher is telling the students that these questions are very important to say correctly when one is asking for help with English vocabulary, so the students should learn to ask these questions correctly. 선생님은 학생들에게 이런 질문들은 영어 어휘에 대한 질문을 할 때 올바르게 표현하는 데 매우 중요하며, 학생들은 이 질문들을 올바르게 하는 것을 배워야 한다고 말하고 있다.

Polite Expression

 공손한 표현에 대해 예를 들어 설명하고 있다. 조동사를 사용한 의문문이 보다 공손하다는 것을 설명하고 있다.

T: When speaking in English, there are certain ways to show politeness.

S1: Could you say that specifically? [1]

T: Okay. Instead of saying, 'Give me the salt', you could ask, 'Would you pass me the salt?' to be polite. Let's think about expressions that show politeness.

S1: How about saying, 'I really appreciate you doing this for me'?

T: Yes, **it's more of a polite answer.** [2] Can you think of anything else?

Tip Lunch vs Luncheon

The formal word for the noon meal, 'luncheon' is really a long form of the original but less formal word 'lunch'. (점심식사의 공식적인 표현인 'luncheon'(점찬)은 일상적인 'lunch'에서 유래된 것이다.)

Expressions used

1) **Could you say that specifically?** : You should say 'Could you be more specific?' or 'What specifically do you mean?'. The student is asking for a clearer answer or an explanation of something.
   'Could you be more specific?' 또는 'What specifically do you mean?'이라고 표현해야 한다. 학생이 보다 분명한 답이나 설명을 요청하고 있다.

2) **it's more of a polite answer** : It's a more polite answer.
   그것이 보다 공손한 대답이다.

Yes or No

'Yes'와 'No'

 'Yes'와 'No'의 용법에 대한 설명이다. 또한 'OK'도 공손하지 못한 표현이므로 바꾸어 표현할 것을 지시하고 있다.

T: Does anyone have a question? No?

S: Yes, we have no question.

T: Yes? If you don't have any questions, you should answer 'no'. Saying 'yes' means that you do have a question.

S: OK.

T: Not, OK. It's too informal you should say **'I got it or I see'**.[1]

S: I see.

Tip Prefixes: 'il', 'im', 'in', and 'ir'
The prefixes 'il-', 'im-', 'in-', 'ir-' are all used to form the negative of various words: illogical, improbable, indigestable, or irresponsible. However, they are not interchangeable. Check the spelling in your dictionary if you're not sure which prefix to use. (접두어 'il-', 'im-', 'in-', 'ir-'은 모두 여러 가지 단어의 부정형을 만들기 위해 사용된다. 그러나 그것들은 교차하여 사용할 수 없다. 어떤 접두어를 사용해야 할지 모르면 사전에서 스펠링을 확인하라.)

Expressions used

1) **I got it, I see**: OK. 알았습니다.

Oily

입에 발린

 선생님의 말씀을 잘 따르는 학생을 적절하게 표현하는 방법에 관해 설명한 내용이다. 원어민 선생님의 학생에 대한 칭찬을 냉소적으로 표현하면 매우 실례가 될 수도 있다.

T: (After making a joke) **Sometimes it's really embarrassing when I think a joke is really funny but nobody laughs, but I can always trust Noah.** [1]

Noah: Thank you.

Ss: Woo….

Nicky: Noah is so oily.

Ss: Yeah, oily.

T: No, Noah is very sweet!

Ss: No, no, no.

T: 'Oily' is kind of a Konglish word. **What's an English word for 'oily'?** [2]

Oily

임에 발린

Tip Origin of 'Tide'

The word 'tide' originally meant 'time'. The meaning of the modern word came about because of the rising and falling of the ocean at regular times of the day. ('Tide'[조류]는 원래 '시간'을 의미했다. 매일 일정한 시간에 해류가 상승하고 하강했기 때문에 오늘날의 의미가 나타난 것이다.)

Expressions used

1) **Sometimes it's really embarrassing when I think a joke is really funny but nobody laughs, but I can always trust Noah**: The teacher made a small joke that no one but one student – Noah – understood.

   선생님이 농담으로 한 말을 노아 이외에는 아무도 이해하지 못했다고 말한다.

2) **What's an English word for 'oily'?**: The teacher is asking for a synonym for the Konglish word. Oily is a Konglish word that means 'someone who can't be trusted'. In other words you can say it like the following:

   He is a nice guy. (positive) 그는 멋있는 녀석이다.

   He is a flatterer. 그는 아첨쟁이이다.

   He's a brown noser. (a little negative) 그는 아첨꾼이다.

   He's kiss ass. (negative) 그는 아첨한다.

   He is kissing up to the teacher. 그는 선생님에게 아첨하고 있다.

   선생님은 한국식 영어 표현에 대한 동의어를 묻고 있다. 'Oily'는 '믿을 수 없는 사람'이라는 의미이다. 다른 말로 다음과 같이 표현하는 것이 좋다.

Looks

 남녀 간의 교제에서 가장 고려해야 할 요소에 대한 이야기이다.
유인물에 적힌 특징을 여섯 개 선택하고 그 이유를 설명하는 담화이다.

T: Alright! Guys! What is most important to you in your boyfriend or girlfriend?

Look at the handout sheet and take one minute and make a list with the given words, **which you may number from top first to sixth.** [1] OK?

Ss: (They do what they are told to.)

T: OK! **What is most important to you in your boyfriend or girlfriend?** [2]

S1: Looks.

T: Why?

S1: **Because looks is just better than ugly.** [3]

T: How about you, Mr. Park?

Mr. Park: Looks.

T: Why?

Mr. Park: Because, because I don't like ugly girl.

T: Have you ever had a pretty girlfriend?

Mr. Park: No. (Everyone laughs.)

T: OK! (pointing to the next student) How about you?

S2: Looks. **Because I have my own style.** [4]

T: Only one style?

S2: Aw… yes!

Looks

외모

Expressions used

1) **which you may number from top first to sixth**: The teacher is telling the students to write the characteristics that are most important – first – down to the sixth most important. 선생님은 학생들에게 가장 중요한 1번부터 6번째로 중요한 특징을 쓰라고 말한다.

2) **What is most important to you in your boyfriend or girl-friend?**: What characteristic is most important to you? 여자친구나 남자친구에게서 가장 중요한 것은 무엇입니까?

3) **Because looks is just better than ugly**: The student is using poor English to explain that a good looking person is better than an ugly person (in the sense of boyfriend or girlfriend). 학생이 '(남자친구나 여자친구의 관점에서) 잘생긴 사람이 못생긴 사람보다 좋다'라는 것을 설명하지만 영어 능력이 부족하다.

4) **Because I have my own style**: The student is saying (jokingly) that he has his own unique taste in what he thinks his girlfriend should look like because he himself has a unique personal style. 학생이 자신만의 독특한 개인적인 스타일이 있기 때문에 자신의 여자친구의 외모에 대한 자신만의 특별한 취향이 있다고 (농담조로) 말하고 있다.

Notorious

역사상 평판이 나쁜 사람에 대한 이야기이다. 역사에서 연산군이 악명 높은 군주인 이유를 구체적으로 설명하는 담화이다.

T: Who was the most notorious person in history?

S1: Hitler.

T: Hitler is maybe the most infamous person.

S2: Nero.

T: How about from Korean history?[1]

S1: King Yunsan.

T: Who is that?

S3: 15th century.

T: Wow. A long time ago. Was it Chosun?

Ss: Yes.

S4: He killed his great··· um··· in order to be the king.

T: To become king he killed the king?

S5: Not he kill the king, his grandmother want to kill mother.

T: So his grandmother murdered his mother?

Ss: Not murder···.

S4: His grandmother··· her··· poison give··· uh··· huh··· huh···

T: Difficult to say, isn't it?

S4: Yes.

T: But if his grandmother did this, why isn't she notorious instead of King Yunsan.

S1: Because it was still King Yunsan's control.[2]

T: OK.

Notorious

악명 높은

 Greenhouse Gases

Not all greenhouse gases are produced by burning fossil fuels such as gasoline and coal.
Large amount of methane are produced by termites and cattle digesting cellulose.
(모든 온실 효과가 석유와 석탄과 같은 화석 연료를 태워서 나온 것은 아니다. 상당량의 메탄 가스는 흰개미와 셀룰로즈를 소화하는 가축으로부터 배출된 것이다.)

Expressions used

1) **How about from Korean history?**: The teacher is asking for an example of a notorious person from Korea's history.
   선생님은 한국 역사에서 악명 높은 사람에 대해 묻고 있다.

2) **it was still King Yunsan's control**: The student is trying to explain that King Yunsan is the notorious person (even though his mother committed the crime) because he was in control of Korea at that time. 그 당시 연산군이 조선을 지배하고 있었기 때문에 (비록 그의 엄마가 범죄를 저질렀지만) 그가 악한 사람이라고 학생이 설명하려고 한다.

Life

Unit 7

인생

 인생의 의미에 대한 대화이다. 학생들이 영어 능력이 부족하여 자신의 사고를 체계적으로 표현하는 데 한계를 나타내고 있다.

T: What are you talking about?

S1: Umm…. We can't find out the meaning of life.

T: Wow! The meaning of life? Hmm….

S1: I think life is given by God.

S2: I think life is given by um… science.

T: By science? What do you mean?

S3: It is made by scientific… (looking at another student and whispering in Korean, '현상'?)

S4: **You write it like 'phenomenon'?** [1]

T: Oh! Phenomenon! **Good use of vocabulary.** [2] So what about the meaning of life?

S4: We were discussing about if life is good.

T: You mean if life is 'worth living'?

Ss: Umm… I think so.

T: Aha! So, what did you think?

S5: I think life is worth living long.

T: You mean…?

S6: **You must live long to find out about the real form of life.** [3]

T: I agree with you.

Life 인생

 How to Spread Seeds

Plants use a variety of methods to scatter or spread their seeds. Some seeds, such as those from the maple tree, have wings that carry them on the wind. Others, like the acorns produced by oak trees, are stored or eaten by animals. Some seeds have tiny hooks that stick to the fur of animals, allowing them to 'hitch a ride'.

(식물은 씨를 퍼트리기 위해 여러 가지 방법을 사용한다. 단풍나무 씨는 그것들을 바람에 따라 운반할 것이 있다. 상수리나무의 도토리는 동물이 저장해서 먹는다. 어떤 씨는 동물의 깃털에 달라붙는 작은 갈고리가 있으며, 그것으로 '무임승차'를 한다.)

Expressions used

1) **You write it like 'phenomenon'?** : The student is telling the teacher that the Korean word has a similar meaning to the word 'phenomenon'. 학생이 선생님에게 그 한국어가 단어 'phenomenon'과 유사한 의미를 지니고 있다고 말한다.

2) **Good use of vocabulary** : The teacher is commending the student on his/her choice of vocabulary.
선생님이 학생의 어휘 선택에 대해 말하고 있다.

3) **You must live long to find out about the real form of life** : The student is telling the teacher that he/she believes a person needs to live a long life in order to more fully understand what 'life' means. 학생은 선생님에게 인생의 의미를 충분히 이해하기 위해서는 오래 살 필요가 있다고 말하고 있다. .

Halloween

할로윈데이

 할로윈데이의 의의와 여러 가지 활동에 대한 대화이다. 담화를 시작하기 위해 먼저 영화 'The Exorcist(퇴마사)'에 대한 이야기를 도입하고 있다.

T: We are going to carve pumpkins and watch a horror movie called 'The Exorcist'. What is an exorcist?

S1: It's a person.

T: What does an exorcist do?

S2: Priest.

T: Kind of a priest, but what is the mission?

S1: Make the ghost away.

T: Not a ghost but a devil or a demon.[1] In this movie, there is a girl and the exorcist who tries to get rid of the devil inside the girl. So while you are carving, I'll have the movie on so that you can watch. And also, before you begin, I have some stories about Halloween to read about. Does anyone know why we celebrate Halloween?

S4: I think in my opinion maybe you are very scared about the devil, so you want to get the devil out. So you want ceremonies to take out the devil.

T: The belief is that all of the people who died want to come back to find their body, so we make parties to make loud noises and scare them away.

Ss: Ah⋯.

T: How do we usually celebrate Halloween?[2]

S5: Parties, mask.

Halloween

S2: Masks and a costume.

T: I believe in Seoul they are having Halloween parties tonight, but it's really a big day for the kids. What do the children do on Halloween?

S4: Give me candy.

T: Right, but what do they say, instead of 'give me candy'?

Ss: Hmmm….

T: They go to all the neighbors' houses and they ring the doorbells with the costume on.

S1: If you don't give me candy, I'll enter your house!

Ss: Hahaha….

T: I will do what if you don't give me candy?

S1: Uh, going to your home?

T: Um… not into the home, but they play some kind of a trick, so they say 'trick or treat'. It means give me a treat or I'll give you a trick.

Ss: Ah….

T: It's for young children, so they take eggs and throw eggs at people, and they throw toilet paper at trees.

S6: Ah… Throw eggs… Hmmm to whom?

T: To anybody.

S4: Hahaha… to everybody.

T: OK. This is something to read about Halloween. David, can you read for us please? (David finishes reading.)

S6: You said that in high school students usually throw the eggs and….

T: Yes.

S6: Where do they do, in school?

T: Most of them in the streets.

S6: I think that if there is a woman who they like, who he likes, he'll throw it to her.

T: Haha. Usually they do that to somebody they don't like.

Tip Past vs Passed

Take care not to confuse 'past' with 'passed'. 'Past' is an adjective, adverb, preposition, or noun as in: We walked past the store. It can also be a noun: That's all in the past. 'Passed' is the past tense of the verb, to pass, as in: A week passed after he went to America. ('Past' 와 'passed'를 혼동하지 않도록 하세요. 'Past'는 형용사, 부사, 전치사, 또는 명사로 사용됩니다. 'Passed'는 동사 'pass'의 과거시제입니다.)

Expressions used

1) **Not a ghost but a devil or a demon** : The teacher is telling the students that an exorcist does not get rid of ghosts; an exorcist gets rid of devils and/or demons. 선생님은 학생들에게 퇴마사는 유령을 제거하는 것이 아니라 마귀나 악마를 제거한다고 말하고 있다.

2) **How do we usually celebrate Halloween?** : The teacher is asking the students how Halloween is celebrated. 선생님은 학생들에게 할로윈데이는 어떻게 거행되느냐고 묻고 있다.

Time Flies

시간은 날아간다

 관용어를 사용하여 일상적인 생활을 표현하는 방법을 학습하고 있다.
여기서는(Time Flies)가 담화에 이용되고 있다.

T: Now, practice the expressions with your partners.

S1: How was your weekend?

S2: Good. How about you?

S1: Good.

T: Hey, don't just say, 'Good'. **Use the expressions we learned today.** [1]

S1: Did you have a great time when you went to Seoul?

S2: Yes. I met my close friends. I realized that time flies when I met them.

T: Very good. Let's wrap up now. Please memorize all the idioms we've learned because **they will be on the test.** [2] Good luck on your tests!

 Prefix 'co'
The prefix 'co' gives a sense of 'together': People who cooperate (sometimes spelled with a hyphen, co-operate, work together). (접두사 'co'는 '함께'라는 의미가 있다.: 협력하는 사람은 함께 일한다.)

Expressions used

1) **Use the expressions we learned today**: The students learned new idioms. The teacher is telling the students to practice using them. 학생들은 새로운 관용구를 배웠다. 선생님은 학생들에게 그것들을 사용해서 연습하라고 말한다.

2) **they will be on the test**: The idioms the students learned will be on the test. 학생들이 학습한 관용구가 시험에 출제될 것이다.

Future Goal

 선생님이 인생 목표와 미래의 직업을 혼동하지 않도록 설명하고 있다. 현무라는 학생이 직업과 인생 목표를 혼동하자 선생님이 수정한 후에 다시 발표하도록 지시하고 있다.

T: Today, we will talk about future goals in life. Hyunmoo, what kind of a person do you want to become later on in your life?

Hyunmoo: Well, I am going to be a famous officer. I want to be the captain of Lee Sun Shin, the greatest Destroyer in Korea.

T: I think that **many of you are having a hard time distinguishing the two, future goal in life and future job.** [1] The job you will be having in the future may be a part of your future goal. However, that is not everything. Future goal can be something more philosophical. Hyunmoo, **can you please restate what you have said, including the philosophies in your life?** [2]

Hyunmoo: Yes, to say it once again, I want to be a very generous captain of a battleship. I want the people I work with to be happy. I want the soldiers in my ship to be happy by guaranteeing them free time and suitable living conditions. Even until today, many soldiers live under irrational conditions and suffer from ridiculous orders from their seniors. There is no system and regulations to support the rights and happiness of soldiers in Korea.

T: Very good point! Wow! Hyunmoo, your English has improved greatly! Keep up the good work···. Would anyone else like to speak out?

Minhyuk: I would. I want to be an ocean biologist. I want to make research on the natural habitats of the ocean. We have very little information of the ocean especially the deep ocean. I want to benefit from the science, so that our country would be richer and more advanced.

John: Excellent!

Tip Origin of 'Brandy'

'Brandy' is the shortened form of a Dutch word, 'brandewijn', meaning 'burnt wine'. In fact the wine was not burned but distilled over a fire. ('Brandy'[브랜디]는 네덜란드 어인 '불에 탄 술[포도주]를 의미하는 brandewijn'의 단축형이다. 사실 그 술은 불에 태운 것이 아니라 불로 증류한 것이다.)

Expressions used

1) **many of you are having a hard time distinguishing the two, future goal in life and future job**: The teacher is telling the students that they are confusing the meanings of 'goal in life' with 'what your (the students') future job will be'. 선생님은 학생들이 인생의 목표와 미래에 가질 직업의 의미를 혼돈하고 있다고 말한다.

2) **can you please restate what you have said, including the philosophies in your life?**: The teacher is asking the student to say again, in clearer English, what he/she just said, but this time include your (the students') personal philosophies on life. 선생님이 학생에게 보다 명백하게 그리고 이번에는 인생에 대한 개인적인 철학을 포함하여 다시 말하기를 요청하고 있다.

Talking

 학습 목적을 말한 뒤에 각자 상대방을 알기 위해 개인적인 질문을 하는 활동이다. 특히 실수에 대해 부끄럽게 여기지 말고 자유롭게 말할 것을 권유하고 있다.

T: Pop quiz! It's a test day!

Ss: What? No! Why?

T: Haha, **got ya! Just kidding!** [1]

Ss: Whew!!

T: It's a conversation class. You are all language majors, so I am hoping that you students have fewer problems. As I said, it's a conversation class. **What is the main target for this class?** [2]

S1: Talking.

S2: Listening.

T: Good, what else?

S3: Shy?

T: What do you mean by 'shy'? Do you mean not to feel shy in conversation class?

S3: Yes.

T: Alright, talking is one task. Talking is one of the 'class participation' parts. Get involved with class, and **by the end of the semester you will see the development within you.** [3] You should not feel shy or bad when making mistakes while you are talking. I am here to correct your English. Therefore, exploring a new vocabulary, sentence structure, trying to use as much English as possible and most importantly, to use appropriate words⋯. What do I mean by 'appropriate'? Somebody tell me?

S2: High class English?

T: High class English? Do you mean a term of respect? I will set you an example. To you people, I can say 'Hello, guys', 'How are you doing' or 'What's up?' But when I meet the Superintendent of the school, I should not use those sentences, though I will use terms of respect by saying, 'Hello, Sir'. Do you understand?

Ss: Aha!

T: Alright, **we are on the right track.** [4] Let's get going. For today's class I must hear your speaking ability. It's going to be a 'get to know each other'. You know a lot about your classmates, but do you know them outside of school, before you guys met each other?

Ss: **No, not enough!** [5]

T: Well, **there you go.** [6] This class will get you to speak by asking at least two questions, and, as well as that, you will know much more about your classmate.

S3: We ask any questions?

T: No!! It is, 'Can we ask any questions?' Full structured sentence, alright?

S3: Sorry, John!

T: Alright, pay attention lads! Never say sorry in my class when you make a mistake. It is very normal to make mistakes as it's not your first language. I often make

English mistakes although I am Canadian! OK?

Ss: OK, John!

T: Cool. Let's begin the question. Who wants to ask whom a question?

Expressions used

1) **got ya!** : A-ha! I was only joking! 아하! 농담이야!

2) **What is the main target for this class?** : The teacher is asking what the main point or objective is.
선생님은 요점이나 목적이 무엇인지 묻고 있다.

3) **by the end of the semester you will see the development within you** : The teacher is telling the students that after one full semester, they will see an improvement in their English ability.
선생님은 학생들에게 한 학기가 끝난 뒤에는 영어 능력이 향상된 것을 알게 될 것이라고 말하고 있다.

4) **we are on the right track** : 'On the right track' is an idiom which means one is following the correct course of action. In this case, the students are beginning to understand how English shows respect without special honorific language. 'On the right track'(잘 진행되고 있는)은 올바른 과정을 따르고 있다는 것을 의미하는 관용어이다. 이 경우 학생들이 특별한 존칭어 없이도 영어로 경의를 표현할 수 있는 방법을 이해하기 시작하는 것이다.

5) **No, not enough!** : The students are telling the teacher that they don't know enough about their classmates lives outside of the Naval Academy. 학생들은 그들이 학교 밖에서의 급우들의 생활을 모른다고 선생님에게 말하고 있다.

6) **there you go** : In this situation, the students have verified the point that the teacher just made.
이 경우 학생들은 선생님이 말한 요점을 확인해 준 것이다.

Current Issues

시사 문제에 대한 토의 제목을 설정하고, 그룹별 토의를 실시하도록 지시하고 있다. 그룹당 6명으로 자유롭게 토론 주제를 정해 토의할 것을 지시하고 있다.

T: We are going to talk about current issues.

Who will suggest something first? [1]

S1: I would like to talk about 2008 Beijing Olympics.

T: Are there any ideas?

S2: What about the politics?

T: It's up to you. Please get into groups of 6 and discuss with your classmates the current issue.

S1: Okay.

Tip Prefixes: 'inter-' vs 'intra-'

Be careful not to confuse the two prefixes 'inter-' meaning 'between' and 'intra-' meaning 'within'. Think of the internet, a system of connected computers around the world, and 'intranet' which is a system of connected computers, usually within a company.

('between'을 의미하는 접두어 'inter-'와 'within'을 의미하는 접두어 'intra-'를 혼동하지 마세요. 세계의 컴퓨터 시스템인 '인터넷'과 대개 회사 안의 연결된 컴퓨터인 '인트라넷'을 생각해 보세요.)

Expressions used

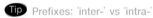

1) **Who will suggest something first?** : Who will be the first to suggest a topic of discussion? 누가 처음으로 토의 주제를 제안하겠어요?

Water Sports

수상 스포츠

 주말에 학생들이 과외 활동으로 한 수상 스포츠 '카누와 카약'에 대한 이야기이다. 학생들에게 수상 활동을 직접 묘사하게 하여 다양한 담화를 유도하고 있다.

T: Good morning. How are you today?

Ss: Good morning.

T: Last week, you had water sports. How was it?

Ss: Very exciting.

T: I can't hear you.

Ss: Exciting. Interesting.

T: What did you do, Sumin?

Sumin: I play canoeing.

T: We don't say 'play canoeing'. We went canoeing. Repeat. We went canoeing.

Sumin: We went canoeing.

T: What did you do?

S: We had kayaking.

T: You went kayaking? Who also went kayaking?

S: I did.

T: How was kayaking?

S: Fun.

T: How did you go kayaking?

S: Peddle.

T: (Writes on the board.) peddle/paddle. Not peddle, paddle. Kilsu, what did you do?

Kilsu: I did yacht.

T: You went yachting? Who else went yachting?

S: I went yachting.

T: Did you do yachting well? Was there any problem? Was the wind good?

S: I fall in.

T: You fell in? You fell into the water! If the boat tips over, how do you get the boat back up again?···. **Help me. Try.** [1]

S: (Nobody speaks.)

T: **Can you demonstrate?** [2] Show me. Stand up. Draw it on the board.

S: (Draws the picture on the board. Dagger를 당기는 모습을 취한다.)

T: Oh, pull the dagger. That's good.

All of you back again? I'm glad. Did you prepare your project?

S: Two weeks later.

T: No, two weeks from now. Half of the time already has passed.

Expressions used

1) **Help me. Try**: The teacher does not fully understand what a student is trying to say. He/she is encouraging the student to try and say something correctly.
선생님은 학생이 말하려고 하는 것을 충분히 이해하지 못했다. 그는 학생이 어떤 사실을 정확히 표현하게끔 격려해 주고 있다.

2) **Can you demonstrate?**: Can you show me what you mean?
너의 의도를 몸짓으로 표현해 보겠니?

관계대명사를 이용하여 영화와 배우들에 대해 논평하는 연습이다. 그룹별로 5분만에 영화나 영화배우 또는 감독에 대해 관계절을 이용하여 세 가지 논평을 만들 것을 지시하고 있다.

T: What was the theme of our last week's topic? It was movies. Take a look at our New Interchange book. Here we use the relative clauses such as which, that, who, to describe a movie.

T: Did you enjoy the new novel from Steven King?

S: Yes. It was an excellent novel which was hard to put down.

T: Excellent. Who's Steven Spielberg?

S: He is a famous movie director who made one of the most successful movies of all time.

T: Good. Who is Tom Cruise?

S: Tom Cruise is one of the richest actors who was married to Nichole Kidman.

T: OK. What about Walt Disney?

S: Walt Disney was a famous movie director who was very popular with children.

T: Alright. Now, what I want you to do is to get into groups and make three more ideas. I'll give you five minutes.

S: What about?

T: What does it have to be about? [1] Could be about sports, art, play, acting, music, and so on···.

(A few minutes later)

T: **When we come back,** [2] we are going to do a movie review. A 'critic' is a person who reviews movies. Summarizing the story, criticizing or praising the movie···. So, basically you guys are becoming critics.

Tip Main clause vs Subordinate clause
There are two types of clauses in grammar. A main clause stands alone and form a complete sentence, e.g. 'I switched on the light'. A subordinate clause cannot stand on its own and has to go with a main clause to form a sentence, e.g. 'I switched on the light when it got dark'.
(문법에는 두 종류의 절이 있다. 주절은 단독으로 사용되며, 완전한 문장을 형성한다. 에. '나는 불을 켰다.' 종속절은 단독으로 사용될 수 없으며, 주절과 함께 문장을 형성한다. 에. '어두워진 뒤에 나는 불을 켰다.')

Expressions used

1) **What does it have to be about?** : The student is asking the teacher what the discussion topic should be about.
학생이 선생님에게 토의 주제는 무엇에 대한 것인지 묻고 있다.

2) **When we come back** : When we return from our ten-minute break
우리가 10분간 휴식을 마친 다음에는

Making Sentences with 'If'

'If' 조건절 만들기

 주어진 'If' 조건절 다음에 이어질 말을 만들어 문장을 완성하라는 지시다.
주절을 미래로 표현할 것을 지시하고 있다.

T: OK! Make a sentence with; 'If I get a part time job'. (Pointing to Minhi) **Why don't you start first?** [1]

Minhi: If I get a part time job, I will… I will work hard.

T: OK. Next. Mr. Lee!

Mr. Lee: If I get a part time job, I… 모….

T: If I get a part time job?

Mr. Lee: I will buy new clothes.

T: Good! Mr. Park! It's your turn!

Mr. Park: If I get a part time job, I have to buy a present for my parents.

T: No. **You need to say** [2] 'I will have to buy a present for my parents'. OK?

Mr. Park: OK.

S2: Again! (Everyone laughs.)

T: Yeah! Good idea! Why don't you say that again?

Mr. Park: OK. Ah… if I get a part time job, I will have to buy a present for my parents.

T: Good job!

Apostrophe

You make the possessive form of a singular noun by adding apostrophe 's' at the end: my friend's book. Plural nouns have 's' apostrophe at the end: my friends' help. (아포스트로피 에스 ('s)를 끝에 추가하여 단수명사의 소유격을 만든다. : 내 친구의 책. 복수명사는 끝에 에스+아포스트로피(s')를 가진 다. : 내 친구들의 도움.)

Expressions used

1) **Why don't you start first?** : The teacher is telling this student to go first. 선생님이 이 학생에게 먼저 시작하라고 지시하고 있다.

2) **You need to say** : The teacher is making a correction to something a student said incorrectly. 선생님이 학생이 잘못 말한 것에 대해 수정 하고 있다.

상황에 따라 자기를 지칭하는 표현이 다르다는 것을 설명하고 있다.
특히 상대방에게 인사를 할 때에는, 반드시 상대방의 이름을 덧붙이는
것이 공손하다는 점을 강조하고 있다.

T: I want to ask you, when you're identifying yourself, when you're introducing yourself, what is the difference between 'I'm', 'it's', and 'this is'?

Ss: ….

T: When should I use 'it's'?

S4: It's calling.

T: You can use it for calling and writing. What about 'It's Nina'?

S2: Introducing.

T: Introduce, but it's more formal compared to 'this is', but it's the same meaning. What about 'I'm Nina'? When do you use 'I'm'? **This is a mistake you make often.** [1] We only use 'I'm Nina' the first time you meet somebody.

Ss: Oohhh.

T: Yeah, only the first time. In your e-mails, most of you said, 'I'm'. So, next time, you can say 'this is' in the e-mails, and when you call me on the phone, you should say 'it's'. Most of the time, you don't use your names, but your titles instead, **but it's a very uncomfortable situation** [2] when you don't remember a person's name in the US. But it's very polite to use the person's name many times when you're speaking to them. It's more polite to say, 'Hello, Jude' instead of just, 'Hello'.

Tip Prefix, 'Re-'

The prefix 're-' is usually spelt with a hyphen before a word that begins with an 'e', such as 're-enlist', or if it could be confused with another word: to re-form means to form again, but to reform is to make or become better. (접두사 're-'는 주로 're enlist'와 같이 'e'로 시작하는 단어 앞에는 하이픈을 사용한다. 그렇지 않을 경우 다른 단어와 혼동될 우려가 있다.: 're-form'은 재조직하다라는 의미지만, 'to reform'은 개량하다는 뜻이다.)

Expressions used

1) **This is a mistake you make often**: 'You' is plural here. 'This is a mistake that you, the students, often make.'
   여기에서 'you'는 복수이다. 이것은 여러분들이 종종 저지르는 실수이다.

2) **it's a very uncomfortable situation**: Not remembering a person's name during a conversation with them is uncomfortable.
   대화 중에 상대방의 이름을 기억하지 못하는 것은 불편하다.

Cultural Discrimination

 외국인에 대한 문화적 차별을 고쳐야 한다는 내용이다. 특히 국내에
거주하는 동남아 노동자들의 인권 침해를 금지해야 한다는 주장이다.

T: Continuing from last week, let's discuss more about
different cultures. Although the world is becoming more
globalized in recent times, many of us still do not fully
understand the differences among various cultures. Who
will start out by explaining why we have to be careful
towards other people from different parts of the world?

Jiyoung: Well, I think that Koreans are very kind to foreigners. **People are always ready to be well to other country
people.** [1]

T: **First of all, you have misunderstood my question!** [2] I was
not asking your opinion about the behavior of Koreans to
people from other countries. Also, you should have used
the term 'foreigners' instead of 'other country people'.

Jiyoung: Oh! Sorry, I will say it again. I think that people
must be careful not to insult religion, politics, and other
sensitive things that might get foreigners angry. I would not
like it if a foreigner said bad things about kimchi or Admiral
Lee Sun Shin.

T: Very good point! We should not make fun of or criticize
about things we are not sure of. Especially other cultures
and things that are sensitive such as religious and political
matters. Would anyone else like to try?

Hyunil: Yes, I do. I want to say an example. Koreans should not be so bad and mean to workers from Southeast Asia. Countries like Philippines, Indonesia, Thailand, and Pakistan. These people are very poor and they come to Korea for money. They work hard but **Korean people so bad treat them.** [3] They even hit them, it is very bad and cruel. We should not let this happen. Some people even make fun of their skin color and food. We should not do this.

T: Well said! We should respect other people and other cultures, not make fun of or criticize them. People must be aware that understanding and respecting foreign culture is the first step towards world peace. I am glad that many of you know that and hope you practice what you know.

Expressions used

1) **People are always ready to be well to other country people**:The student is using poor English. He/she is trying to say that Korean people usually try to treat foreigners well. 학생의 영어 표현이 서툴다. 그/그녀는 한국 사람들이 대개 외국인을 잘 대우하고 있다고 말하려 한다.

2) **First of all, you have misunderstood my question!**:The teacher is telling the student that he/she misunderstood the question that was asked. 선생님은 학생이 질문을 잘못 해석하고 있다고 말하고 있다.

3) **Korean people so bad treat them**:Poor English. The student is trying to say that 'Korean people often treat some foreigners poorly and with disrespect' or 'Korean people treat them so badly'. 서툰 영어. 학생은 '한국인이 종종 외국인을 불손하게 대우한다' 또는 '한국인은 외국인에 대한 처우가 나쁘다'고 말하려 한다.

[Cartoon] A Drugstore

My Family

가족에 대한 사랑이 중요한 이유와 우리나라의 휴일에 대한 이야기이다.
선생님은 가족에 대한 비방은 금지하고 있다.

T: **Continuing from last time,** [1] We will talk about the importance of family and relatives. Most of us have family and relatives. Who does not have any family or relatives?

Ss: Nobody! We all have family and relatives.

T: Alright, then, first of all, can anyone tell me why family is important?

S1: Family is important because family loves you. Family can die for me and I can die for my family.

T: Do you mean that the members in your family love and care for each other?

S1: Yes, absolutely! That's why I can death for family.

T: You mean you could die for your family, not death. Hyun Joon, who is the favorite person among your family and please also tell us why.

Hyun Joon: My favorite is my mother. She loves me a lot and raised me until I was 19 years old.

T: Anyone else? Okay, Minhyuk.

Minhyuk: I don't like my grandmother. She do bad thing to Mother.

T: Umm… Minhyuk, I meant the favorite member in your family, not the ones you don't like. Besides, your grandmother would be very upset to hear this, wouldn't she?

Minhyuk: Oh! I am sorry, John. My favorite is grandfather! He is old, but we used to go fishing together and it was very fun.

T: Now, do you remember what we discussed in class last week? We talked about traditional family gatherings such as Thanksgivings and Chuseok.

Ss: Yes, we remember.

T: Who wants to explain to me what you do on Chuseok?

Insoo: I will tell you! On Chuseok we play with our relatives. We play traditional card games and stick games. We also eat good food! Very delicious!!

T: Alright…. What about other holiday ceremonies? Anything else?

Hyunmin: I will tell you about Hangul! It was invented by Sejong King in Chosun a long time ago! So it is great!

T: **What are you talking about?** [2] I did not ask for an explanation of Hangul. I want you to tell me about traditional Korean holidays, and what you do during that time. Nice try, but please try again.

My Family

기족

Expressions used

1) **Continuing from last time**: The teacher is telling the class that they are going to continue in this class what they probably didn't finish in the previous class. 선생님은 그들이 이전 시간에 끝마치지 못한 것을 이번 시간에 계속할 것이라고 말하고 있다.

2) **What are you talking about?**: The student is not answering the question the teacher asked, so the teacher is asking him/her what he/she is talking about. 학생이 선생님이 묻는 질문에 답하지 않고 있다. 따라서 선생님이 그에게 무슨 말을 하는지 묻고 있다.

Role

교과서에 나오는 대화문을 보고 읽기 연습을 하기 위해 역할을 지명하고 있다. 지원자가 없자 선생님이 독려하는 표현이 인상적이다.

T: Who will be Mr. Lee? Who is very brave? Nobody? **Come on. Don't you have the guts?** [1]

S1: I'll be Mr. Lee.

T: Thank you. But Mr. Lee is very old. Who wants to be Karen?

S2: I want!

T: Alright! Are you ready, Mr. Lee? Are you ready, Karen? Three, two, one. Action!

 Roll vs Role

Be careful about the spellings of 'roll' and 'role'. A roll is something that is rolled up, including the round shape of bread. The actor's part of somebody's position is spelt 'role', as in 'role-play' or 'role model'. This word comes from French, and is often still spelled in the French way with a circumflex, 'rôle'. (단어 'roll'과 'role'의 철자에 유의하시오. roll(말아서 만든 것)은 둥근 형태의 빵을 포함해 말아서 만든 것이다. 어떤 위치에 대한 배우의 역할은 'role-play'(역할극), 또는 'role model'(모범이 되는 사람)처럼 'role'(역할)이라고 쓴다. 이것은 불어에서 유래되었으며 아직도 불어식으로 굽은 악센트가 있는, 'rôle'로도 종종 쓰인다.)

Expressions used

1) **Come on. Don't you have the guts?** : The teacher is playfully challenging the students. 'Have the guts' means to be brave enough to do something. 선생님이 학생들에게 농담으로 도전적인 말을 하고 있다. '배짱이 있다'는 말은 무언가를 시도해 볼 정도로 용감하다는 의미이다.

Requests in American or British English

Unit 20

요청하는 表現의 차이

이 자료는 Ann Malamah-Thomas(1987)에 수록된 '요청 또는 요구를 위한 적절한 표현'을 찾기 위한 대화이다. 대화문에서는 상대방에게 담배와 담뱃불을 빌리고 싶으면 어떤 식으로 표현해야 할 것인가를 설명하고 있다. 먼저 영국식 영어로 표현된 원문을 정리하고, 다음으로 이를 미국 원어민 선생님이 일상적인 미국식 영어로 개작한 것이다. 두 가지 표현의 차이는 영국식 영어와 미국식 영어의 차이뿐만 아니라 교수법 연구에도 참고가 될 것이다. 또한 이 글은 의사소통식 언어 교육(communicative language teaching)으로 학습을 시키는 선생님의 진지한 노력이 잘 드러나는 담화이다.

A. Request in British English — I want to smoke

T: OK, Kilsu you are walking down the street with Mr. Lee. You are very good friends. OK? You want to smoke but you don't have anything. What, what do you say to Mr. Lee?

Kilsu: Um, er, could you passing me… er… one cigarette, please?

T: I don't think so. I don't think so.

Kilsu: Do you think… I want a cigarette.

T: OK, you could say I want a cigarette and what would you say Mr. Lee?

Mr. Lee: Of course. Here, here you are.

T: OK, so he gives you a cigarette Kilsu and now you want something else. So, what do you ask for now?

Ss: Matches, matches.

T: Yeah, but you don't say matches or fire. (laugh.)

What do you ask him?

S: Er··· can you please··· er··· give me fire?

T: Fire.

S: Give me.

T: A light, yes. We say 'a light' in English. So we'd say 'Can you please give me a light' or···.

S: Have you got any matches?

T: Have you got any matches? OK.

B. Request in American English — I Want to smoke

T: OK. Kilsu you are walking down the street with Mr. Lee. You are good friends. OK? Now, you want to smoke but you don't have anything. What, what do you say to Mr. Lee?

Kilsu: Um, er, could you passing me··· er··· one cigarette, please?

T: I don't think so. I don't think so.

Kilsu: I want a cigarette?

T: I want a cigarette? Oh, it has a different meaning. It means that I want to smoke here or I want a break to smoke a cigarette. For example, if you are thirsty, you can say, 'I want water'. It means I will have water.

Kilsu: Do you have a cigarette?

T: Almost. **You can be a little more polite.**[1] Can…

Kilsu: Can I have a cigarette?

T: Right. Or you can say in other words… Sujin?

Sujin: May I have a cigarette?

T: Then, what would you say, Mr. Lee?

Mr. Lee: Sure, here you are.

T: Good. Or you can say…?

Mr. Lee: Here it is.

T: OK, so he gives you a cigarette. Kilsu, now **you need something else to smoke.**[2] So, what can you ask for now?

Ss: Matches, matches.

S3: Matches? Fire?

T: Yeah, but we don't say matches or fire. What do you say when you need matches?

S4: Er… can you please… er… give me fire?

T: No, not fire.

S5: Give me light.

T: Give me a light. We say 'a light'. But you shouldn't ask him. You can say it a little more politely. So we should say 'Do….

S5: Do you got any light?

T: No, we don't say any light.

S6: Do you have a light?

T: Good. Do you have a light… or… can I use/borrow a light? Also, you can say…? Have…?

S7: Have you got a light?

T: Have you got a light? OK. Now repeat after me; Have you got a light? Now practice the dialogue in pairs, with your partner.

 Snorkel

'Snorkel' comes from the German 'Schnorchel', which was originally a dialect word meaning 'nose' or 'mouth'. ('스노클'은 코 또는 입을 의미하는 독일어 방언인 'Schnorchel'에서 유래된 것이다.)

Expressions used

1) **You can be a little more polite** : The teacher is telling the student that he/she could speak more politely.
   선생님은 학생에게 더 공손히 말하라고 지시하고 있다.

2) **you need something else to smoke** : The teacher is telling the student that something else beside a cigarette is necessary; you also need something to light the cigarette with. 선생님은 학생에게 담배 외에 다른 어떤 것이 필요하다고 말하고 있다. 담배에 불을 붙일 것이 필요하다.

[Cartoon] Calling a Cab

Screen Calls

전화를 선별하다

'응답기'를 사용하는 이유와 '응답기'에 남겨둘 적절한 메모에 관한 이야기이다. 학생들이 명확히 질문의 요점을 이해하지 못하자 선생님이 계속 일방적으로 수업을 진행하는 상황이다. 처음 학생들이 'screen calls'의 의미를 모르자 질문을 다양하게 전환하고 있다. 질문의 전환(rephrasing)과 질문의 단순화(simplification)에 대한 참고 자료로 이용할 수 있다.

T: Open your idiom books, page 33.

(All clear! Idiom in context by H. K. Fragiadakis, Book2, 1993)

Question 1 :

Do you have an answering machine? If yes, do you like having it? Do you ever 'screen' calls? Tell the others what your greeting says. If you don't have any answering machine, would you like to get some day? Why or why not? If you had a machine, what would your greeting be?

....

T: What does this mean, 'screen calls'? In English. No writing.

Ss: (No answer)

T: You listen to his/her speaking on the phone but you don't say anything. **When would you screen calls?** [1]

Ss: (No answer)

T: OK. If you have an answering machine, what would your message say?

Ss: (No answer)

T: (On the board)

I'm not at home now but if you leave a message after the beep I will call you.

T: What's wrong with this message? This is bad. What's wrong with that? Why is that not good? (He circles the clause, 'I'm not at home.') Why is that bad information? No English writing.

Ss: (No answer)

T: (On the board) I can't come to the phone.

T: Why is this better? Why is this better than the first one?

Ss: (No answer)

T: When you say, 'I'm not at home' it means I am out of the house. Then, whoever is calling knows your house is empty and could steal stuff.

Ss: (No answer)

T: What would your message be in your dormitory? [2] Many people leave a very basic message. But I used to play jokes. When someone calls and says, 'hello', my answering machine says; Ha, I'm taking a shower, so I'm naked. So, leave your message and I'll call back after the shower. I'll give you 5 minutes. You should make a message on your answering machine in pairs.

Ss: (No answer)

T: Now question two; What would you do when you call a person or place that has an answering machine and you have to speak English? Do you ever hang up and write down what you want to say?

 **Tip** Origin of 'Kindergarten'
'Kindergarten' comes from the German word, 'kind'(child) and 'garten'(garden)—so its original meaning was 'children's garden'. ('유치원'은 독일어 'kind'｜어린이｜와 'garten'｜정원｜에서 나온 것이다. 그래서 그것의 원래 의미는 '어린이의 정원'이다.)

Expressions used

1) **When would you screen calls?**: 'Screen calls' means to use an answering machine to listen to who is calling before deciding whether or not to answer the phone. '전화를 선별하다'는 전화를 받을 것인 가를 결정하기 전에 누가 전화하는지를 듣기 위해서 응답기를 사용한다는 의미이다.

2) **What would your message be in your dormitory?**: If you lived in the dormitory and you had a telephone answering machine, what message would you record?
만약 당신이 기숙사에 거주하고 응답기가 있으면, 어떤 메시지를 남겨둘 것인가?

[Cartoon] Telephone Conversation

Rules of Presentation

 발표 시간, 반론, 채점 기준에 대한 설명이다. 먼저 주제를 소개하고 내용을 발표하라고 말한 후, 발표를 마친 다음에는 반박과 방어 활동을 할 것을 지시하였다.

A. Time (시간)

T: **If you are less than 3 minutes, minus a point.** [1]

S: More than 3 minutes?

T: **Over is okay.** [2] If you speak 2 minutes and 55 seconds, that's okay. But if you speak 2 minutes and 30 seconds, probably -1 point. If you speak 2 minutes -2 points. Clear? Captains. Are your teams ready?

S1: Yes.

T: Okay. **Introduction, start!** [3]

Expressions used

1) **If you are less than 3 minutes, minus a point**: In this situation, the teacher is explaining to the students that speaking for less than 3 minutes will result in the students having one point deducted from their overall grade. 선생님은 3분 이하로 말하면 학생들은 종합 등급에서 1점이 감점될 것이라고 설명하고 있다.

2) **Over is okay**: If you speak for more than three minutes, that's OK. 3분 초과해도 무방하다.

3) **Introduction, start!**: The teacher is telling the student to begin his/her debate introduction. 선생님이 학생에게 토론 도입을 시작하라고 말하고 있다.

B. Rebuttal (논박)

Attacker: Don't you think it is ridiculous…? [1]

Speaker: No, what I want to say is…. [2]

T: Time. Stop. Time is over. I have to control the time. When I say 'stop' or 'time', don't be upset.

Tip Sea or sea

When it is used with names, 'sea' is written with a capital 'S': 'The North Sea'. The biggest sea in the world is the South China Sea, which is part of the Pacific Ocean. The next three biggest are the Caribbean Sea, the Mediterranean Sea, and the Bering Sea.

(이름과 함께 사용하면 'sea'는 대문자 'S'로 쓰인다.: 'The North Sea'. 세상에서 가장 큰 바다는 태평양의 일부인 'the South China Sea'[남중국해]이다. 그 다음 3개는 카리브 해, 지중해, 베링 해이다.)

Expressions used

1) **Don't you think it is ridiculous…?** : The student is asking a rhetorical question meaning that he/she believes some point made in the debate is ridiculous or absurd. 학생은 토론에서 제시된 어떤 사항이 엉터리이고 터무니없지 않느냐고 묻고 있다.

2) **what I want to say is…** : The student is explaining that he/she may not have been clear. 학생은 자신의 말이 분명하지 않았을지 모른다는 것을 설명하고 있다.

C. Grade (채점)

T: This is how you will be graded. First, your speaking time, fluency, intonation, etc. Second, presentation skills will be graded; volume, authority, pace (means speed), looking at the audience, etc. The last part you will be graded on is debate. **Strengthen your reasons, be well organized, which means well prepared.** [1] Lastly, response. Do you defend well or poorly?

Don't ever tell me again you can't speak English. [2] You all spoke brilliantly! Remember what you did today.

Ss: Thank you.

Expressions used

1) **Strengthen your reason, be well organized, which means well prepared :** The teacher is giving the students some guidelines on debate skills. 선생님은 학생들에게 토론 기술에 대한 지침을 주고 있다.

2) **Don't ever tell me again you can't speak English :** The teacher is simply commending the students on their speaking ability. The students always say how they can't speak English very well. The teacher is telling them that they are wrong. 선생님은 단순히 학생들의 표현 능력을 칭찬하고 있다. 학생들은 항상 영어를 잘 못한다고 말한다. 선생님은 그들의 생각이 틀렸다고 말하고 있다.

15년 뒤에 일어날 일에 대해 그룹별로 두 개의 주제를 설정하고, 10분 동안 조건절을 이용하여 대화문을 만들라는 지시이다.

T: We'll begin with 10 minutes discussion. [1] You should have a discussion for 10 minutes. Choose two topics, two free topics, and discuss them for 10 minutes. **It is about what will be going on in Korea 15 years from now.** [2] You can choose any topic…. Now, Group A, Captain Jung, what are your two topics?

Jung: Korea clothing.

T: Oh, Korean fashion. And?

Jung: Health and food.

T: Well-being? Good. What is well-being to Koreans? What does well-being mean to Koreans? **A little bit of Korean, OK.** [3] Now, write the sentences. Korean fashion and well-being. Group B, what will change in the future? Myung-ghi?

Myunghi: (Captain of Group B) Lifestyle will be changed.

T: Lifestyle. And? Keep going, Myunghi. What will happen to you in 15 years?

S: My hair will be white.

T: Then what do you want?

S: I'm going to buy a wig.

T: Then you want your hair to be black once again?

S: That's one thing I'd like to change.

T: OK. In 15 years you'll get a little bit of fat and lots of things will change. Now choose two topics. And make conditional clauses. Don't worry about your grammar. Just speak.

Ss: (Students are writing in groups.)

T: (In 10 minutes) Now, Group A. Read your sentences···.

Any question?

Now, take break time. 10 minutes break.

Expressions used

1) **We'll begin with 10 minutes discussion**: The teacher is telling the students that the first thing they will do in class is have a ten-minute English discussion. 학생들이 수업 중에 할 첫 번째 활동은 10분 영어 토론이다.

2) **It is about what will be going on in Korea 15 years from now**: The teacher is telling the students that the question means, 'What will Korea be like in 15 years?' or 'What will be happening in Korea in 15 years'. 선생님이 학생들에게 질문은 '15년 뒤 한국은 어떨 것인가?' 또는 '15년 뒤 한국에는 어떤 일이 일어날 것인가?'라고 말하고 있다.

3) **A little bit of Korean, OK**: The teacher is telling the students that a little bit of Korean language during the discussion is OK. 선생님이 학생들에게 토의 중 약간의 한국어는 무방하다고 말한다.

Military Service

군 복무에 대한 두 사람의 담화문이다. 선생님이 고의적으로 군 복무를 회피하는 사람은 어떻게 처리할 것인지를 묻고 있다.

T: OK. Let's start our presentation.

S1: Do you think our army force is strong enough? Everyone knows that we are now in war against North Korea. **Our number is not even half of North Korea' number.** [1] Also, there are many specially trained forces that try to invade Korea. Although South Korea says we have good tools we can lose the war.

S2: Even if United States is ally, they are constantly at war in Iraq, and other places in the world. Also, we need the power to defend for ourselves. And to defend ourselves, we need more people in the army.

T: Good presentation so far. But I have a question. Then what about the people who don't go to the army? Would it be not fair to the people who do go?

S1: Um⋯. If you are sick or body is not good, you don't have to go.

T: Yes, I know. But my question is how about the people who are perfectly healthy, but get surgery or pay money to not go, and more?

S2: Yes, **that is a problem that Korea is fighting about today.** [2] It will improve.

T: I see. Please continue.

S2: Korea needs to get stronger because it is surrounded by many powerful countries like China, Japan, and Russia. To defend ourselves, we need more men power. That is why we need mandatory army service. Thank you.

T: Good work! Well done. (clap! clap!)

 Tip Shepherd

The word 'shepherd' is a contraction, or shortening, of the words 'sheep herd' meaning a person who herds [moves, tends] sheep.
('shepherd'[양치기]는 '양을 모으는 사람'을 의미하는 'sheep herd'의 축약어입니다.)

Expressions used

1) **Our number is not even half of North Korea' number** : Our military is half the size of North Korea's military.
   우리의 군대는 북한군의 규모의 반이다.

2) **that is a problem that Korea is fighting about today** : That is a problem facing Korea today. 그것이 오늘날 한국이 당면한 문제이다.

Low Birthrate

 우리나라의 저출산율에 대한 문제점과 해결 방안에 대해 두 사람이 담화문을 발표히는 도중 선생님이 현재의 출산율을 묻고 있다.

S1: Our group's presentation is about the low birthrate in Korea.[1] Low birthrate has become a very serious problem. Without children, the society will age gradually and will not have enough workers.

S2: Let's look through what is causing this problem.[2] First, there is the environmental cause. Compared to many other western countries, Korea doesn't support the growth of children. The money needed to grow one children is very expensive. Second, when you have a baby, there are many disadvantages from work and personal life. **Many people now think that babies are threat to their freedom and life.**[3]

T: Just a second. This is a very interesting presentation, and I have a question. What is the current percentage of birthrate for today?

S2: It is 0.8 percent.

T: I see. Please go on.

S1: So what can we do to solve this problem? There should be an increase of child care center. If there are more child care centers, the parents don't have to worry about their children while working.

S2: Also, we need to change our mind. When woman get pregnant while working in a company, there should be a longer maternity leave. In western countries, normally there is about 1 year period of vacation for the mother, while there is about 2 weeks for the father. But in Korea, there is about half a day.

S1: Finally, government support has to be improved. The government has to give more money to the family with new baby to encourage birth rate.

S2: If we can complete this task, Korea's low birthrate problem will be solved.

T: Excellent presentation! Let's give them a hand. (clap! clap! clap!)

Expressions used

1) **Our group's presentation is about the low birthrate in Korea**: Today we'll be discussing Korea's low birthrate problem which is affecting this country.
오늘 우리는 우리나라에 영향을 주고 있는 한국의 저출산율에 대해 토의할 것이다.

2) **Let's look through what is causing this problem**: Let's take a look at some of the reasons behind this problem.
이 문제의 배후에 있는 몇 가지 이유를 살펴 봅시다.

3) **Many people now think that babies are threat to their freedom and life**: Many people feel that having children will hinder [blocking, preventing] their lives in some way such as reducing their freedom or income. 많은 사람들은 육아가 자유 또는 소득의 축소와 같이 어떤 식으로든 삶을 방해한다고 느낀다.

Part 5

학생들은 질서를 유지하고(지나치게 엄격하지 않고), 공정하며(항상 일정하고, 편애하지 않으며), 명백히 설명하고 도움을 주고, 재미있게 가르치고, 친구처럼 참을성 있는 선생님을 일반적으로 좋아하는 것으로 보고되어 있다.

Writing
쓰기

학습내용 ————
주어진 단어 또는 주제에 대한 글쓰기 연습, 글쓰는 방법, 글쓰기에서 유의해야 할 사항, 글의 구조 등에 대한 이론적인 설명 등을 수록하였다.

추측을 나타내는 부사를 사용하여 문장을 만드는 연습이다. 일반적으로 추측의 의미를 가진 부사는 문두에 위치한다고 설명하는 내용이다.

Greg: Anyone who could make a sentence with perhaps, maybe or probably?

S1: I perhaps will go home this weekend.

Greg: Yeah. **I was waiting for that.** [1] Thank you. Listen. When you guys make a sentence with perhaps or maybe, usually you start the sentence with perhaps or maybe. The subject doesn't come before perhaps or maybe, but after. It is not wrong to begin with the subject, but it's too formal. For example, if you're a prince, you may say, 'It will perhaps rain tomorrow' **because he's royalty.** [2] We usually say, 'Perhaps I will go home this weekend'. Everyone got it?

S2: It was a little bit difficult to tell the difference, but **I think I come to know it better.** [3]

Perhaps

Tip Sentence

A sentence was originally a 'way of thinking', and came from the Latin 'sententis', meaning 'opinion'. (문장은 원래 생각하는 방식이라는 의미로, '의견'을 의미하는 라틴어 'sententis'에서 유래하였다.)

Expressions used

1) **I was waiting for that**: The teacher was expecting that a student would make an incorrect response. In this case, the student said, 'I perhaps…' rather than 'perhaps I…' 선생님은 학생이 틀린 대답을 할 것으로 예측하고 있었다. 이 경우 학생이 'perhaps I…'가 아니라 'I perhaps…'라고 말했다.

2) **because he's royalty**: The teacher is telling the student that "It will perhaps…" is not grammatically incorrect, but it sounds very, very formal and only a royal person would use it. 선생님은 학생에게 "It will perhaps…"가 문법적으로 틀린 것이 아니라, 매우 격식적이어서 왕족이 그렇게 말할 것이라고 말하고 있다.

3) **I think I come to know it better**: The student is attempting to say that he/she understands something a little better. 학생이 좀 더 잘 이해할 것 같다고 말한다.

글의 제목을 올바르게 쓰는 방법에 대한 설명이다. 주제문은 쉽게 시제를 맞추어 쓰고, 구어적으로 표현해서는 안된다는 점을 지적하고 있다.

(Students have written each of their thesis sentences from their vacation writing homework on the board.)

Frank: During my third winter vacation, I spent well the time that was given to me.

Henry: The winter vacation came to me.

Harry: Vacation, maybe everybody feel happy if they hear it.

David: Hi, Nina happy new year.

....

T: Paul, can you please read #1?

Paul: (reads #1.) During my third winter vacation, I spent well the time that was given to me.

T: Did anybody begin a sentence with, 'and', 'but' or 'because'?

Ss: No.

T: No? Nobody did? So #1 was OK. David, read #2 please.

David: (reads # 2.) The winter vacation came to me.

T: OK. **Part of the problem is that students make the sentences too difficult.** [1] Try to make it simple. This homework was about your winter vacation. Usually the actions all happened in the past, so the tense would be in the past. Let's read Harry's sentence for example; Vacation, maybe everybody feel happy if they hear it.

Harry: My mistake.

T: It's OK. Everybody made mistakes. Can you please read the next sentence?

Eric: (reads #4.) 'Hi, Nina happy new year.'

T: This is a very common mistake for students. Try not to speak to the reader. Who spoke to the reader on the board?

David: I did. 'Hi, Nina, happy new year.'

T: Thank you for being well-mannered, but **this shouldn't be on the writing.** [2]

Expressions used

1) **Part of the problem is that students make the sentences too difficult:** The teacher is telling the students that a problem many language learners face when writing is that they try to write complex sentences. Keep it simple. 선생님은 학생들에게 많은 언어 학습자들이 글을 쓸 때 직면하는 문제는 복잡한 문장을 쓰려고 하는 것이라고 말하고 있다. 간단히 쓰십시오.

2) **this shouldn't be on the writing:** The teacher is telling the student that he made a mistake; 'speaking' to the reader (in this case the teacher) is a mistake when writing an essay. 선생님이 학생에게 그가 실수를 했다고 말하고 있다.: 독자에게 '말을 하는 것'은 (여기에서는 선생님) 글을 쓸 때에는 잘못이다.

Coherence

 일관성 있는 글쓰기를 하는 방법에 관해 설명하고 있다. 먼저 선생님이 '일관성(coherence)'의 의미를 묻고, 다음으로 일관성 있는 글쓰기를 위한 4가지 조건을 설명하고 있다.

T: Coherence. What does that mean?

S: It's the nickname of cocaine!

T: Um··· No.

S1: I was just joking.

T: Coherence is a state or situation in which all the parts or ideas fit together well so that they form a united whole.

S2: So. You mean a sentence with no mistake?

T: Well. yes. Something like a perfect sentence, but it's more like a clear, traightforward sentence.

S1: Can you give me an example?

T: I surely will! Look at the two paragraphs. The first paragraph is a paragraph with coherence. And the second paragraph is without coherence. I want you to read through the two paragraphs and tell me the difference. You have 3 minutes.

(3 minutes later)

T: OK! Tell me the differences! **Who wants to go first?** [1] You can go first!

S4: Um··· OK···. In coherence sentence···.

T: Coherence sentence or coherent sentence?

S4: Oh, umm. Coherent sentence?

T: It would be 'coherent' sentence. 'Coherence' is a noun.

'Coherent' would be an adjective. **Because it describes 'sentence' you should use the adjective form.** [2] Therefore, 'coherent' sentence would be correct instead of 'coherence sentence'. Do you understand?

S2: I think so. Is there any more things?

T: You mean any more that you should know about coherence?

S2: Yes.

T: Yes there is. Would everybody take a look at the board please.

Ss: (looking at the board)

T: OK. Mindo?

Mindo: Yeah.

T: Would you please read the 4 ways to achieve coherence?

Mindo: OK. 1. repeating key nouns 2. using pronouns 3. transition signals 4. logical ordering

T: What is 'repeating key nouns'?

S: It is using the same noun.

T: Yes. For example, let's look at the second page. Would you read the first 2 sentences please?

S: OK. 'English has almost become an international language. Except for Chinese, more people speak it than any other language···.'

Coherence

 Semicolon
A semicolon can be used along with commas to separate items in a list in a logical way: You
will need knives, forks and spoons; cups and sauces; and plates, bowls and glasses.
(세미콜론은 논리적으로 열거된 항목들을 분리하기 위해 쉼표와 함께 사용된다. 당신은 칼, 포크, 스푼; 컵과 소
스; 접시와 양푼, 유리잔이 필요할 것입니다.)

Expressions used

1) **Who wants to go first?** : The teacher is asking for a first volunteer
   to answer the teacher's question.
   선생님의 질문에 답할 첫 번째 지원자를 묻고 있다.

2) **Because it describes 'sentence' you should use the adjective
   form** : The teacher is describing the difference between the
   adjective 'coherent' and the noun 'coherence', and how to use
   them correctly. 선생님은 형용사 'coherent'와 명사 'coherence' 간의 차이를 설명
   하고 그것을 올바르게 사용하는 방법을 기술하고 있다.

[Cartoon] The Process of Photosynthesis

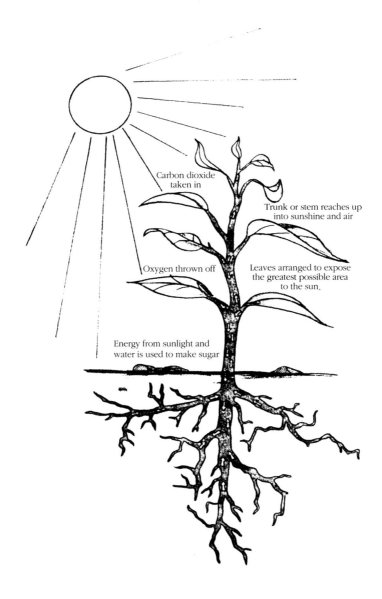

Carbon dioxide
taken in

Trunk or stem reaches up
into sunshine and air

Oxygen thrown off

Leaves arranged to expose
the greatest possible area
to the sun.

Energy from sunlight and
water is used to make sugar

글쓰기의 한 유형인 Brainstorming(즉석 아이디어)을 이용하여 각자 글 쓰는 법을 연습하고 있다. 하나의 주제문과 네 개의 보조문을 쓸 것을 지시하고 있다.

T: Good afternoon! Today we are going to learn outlining. Oh! Before I start, I want to praise everybody because each one of you did your homework. Good job! Most of you wrote in your diary. How many sentences did you write, Mr. Bae?

S1: One.

S2: No, 15 sentences.

T: Good. **It is important to keep on writing.** [1] Now, let's start by looking at the papers I gave you. Now read aloud all together.

Ss: (read)

T: Let's turn over the pages. There are more important things. This is detailed paragraphs and you have to look carefully because you will not have enough time to finish the writing. Do you guys understand?

Ss: ….

T: Take a look at the board. I have done some brainstorming. Now, what I'd like you to do is write a paragraph which includes a topic sentence and supporting sentences. Go ahead, take out your papers and pen to write this down. OK. Mr. Lim, do you have questions?

S: Work in two people?

T: No, do it alone.

S: How many sentences?

T: Look at the board. One, two, three, four sentences to support your main idea.

Ss: (start writing)

T: Some of the English will be difficult but don't get stressed. [2] Find the word that is irrelevant. Mr. Choi, do you understand what we are doing?

Mr. Choi: Yes, we have to check···.

T: All right! You know what you are doing.

Expressions used

1) **It is important to keep on writing:** The teacher is explaining that in 'free writing'(a type of brainstorming activity), students should not stop writing. 선생님은 '자유롭게 쓰기(일종의 생각나는 대로 적는 행위)'에서는 학생들이 글쓰기를 멈추지 않아야 한다고 설명하고 있다.

2) **Some of the English will be difficult but don't get stressed:** The teacher is telling the students that some of the vocabulary and expressions won't be easy at first to understand, but not to worry about that. 선생님은 몇몇 어휘와 표현은 처음에는 이해하기 어렵지만 신경 쓰지 말라고 학생들에게 이야기하고 있다.

Outline of Writing

글의 윤곽

 Brainstorming(즉석 아이디어)을 이용하여 '겨울방학'에 대한 짧은 글을 쓰는 방법에 관한 내용이다. 먼저 아이디어를 찾고, 계획을 세우고, 그 다음에 글을 써야 한다고 설명하고 있다.

T: What does it mean to brainstorm? What does this mean?

Ss: Hmm….

T: **If you have a storm inside your brain what does it mean?**[1]

S2: Only output.

T: **You have a lot of activity in your brain.**[2] The first step of writing a paper is that you need to think. What about step 2? What is an outline?

S3: Choosing…?

S4: To write.

S5: To plan.

T: Eric?

S5: It's a plan to write.

T: Yes. You gave your ideas, you made a plan, so you start writing. For your first draft, you should try to write alone… only with your brain… without dictionaries, without teacher's help. After that, you can get corrections from me or other people. Paul, can you read #1 please?

S6: 'A one page paper should usually have 4 to 5 paragraphs, with an introduction and ending.'

T: Remember that each paragraph needs a strong topic sentence. When I read the first sentence of a paragraph, I should know what the paragraph is about. A paragraph should be sometimes more, or sometimes less, but usually about 4 to 6 sentences. So this week for homework, you will have to write about your winter vacation, so this is an example to help you. Easy, right?

Ss: Yes.

T: When we are writing our first sentence, most of you write the same thing; 'Let me introduce my vacation, let me introduce my hometown⋯', but this is not a good way to start a writing. What's another way we can begin this paper?

Ss: Yes.

T: Yes. Give me an example.

S5: Hmm⋯ I will tell?

T: No. This is the same, Patrick.

Patrick: During winter vacation.

T: OK, during winter vacation, I went to Europe, etc. So right now, before you go, I want you to take out your notebooks⋯. Now, I can see some of you don't have notebooks. What I want you to do is step one of this paper. I want you to make a list of the things you did during the vacation. Make a brainstorming list about the winter vacation. Anything you remember from your vacation; people

you saw, places you went, food you ate, and movies you
saw⋯ the weather⋯.

T: Try not to use dictionaries. After you finish your list, I want
you to go ahead and make your outline. Try and make
outline about how you'll organize your paper. After you
make your outline, show it to me, and you can go.

Tip Period

Sometimes the word 'period' is used at the end of a spoken sentence, meaning 'and that's all there is to it. For example, 'You are not going to the movies, in fact, you're not going out, period'. (때로 단어 'period'는 구어의 마지막에 사용하여 '그 말은 그런 뜻이지.'라는 의미를 가진다. 예를 들면, '너는 극장에 안 갈거지. 사실, 너는 밖에 안 나간다는 뜻이지'.)

Expressions used

1) **If you have a storm inside your brain what does it mean?** : It means that your mind is doing a lot of thinking[your mind is really active]. The teacher is using this as a metaphor to try and explain 'brainstorming' for writing ideas. 이 문장은 당신의 마음이 많은 생각을 한다[당신의 마음이 매우 활동적이다]는 의미이다. 선생님이 글을 쓰는 데 있어 'brainstorming'을 설명하기 위해 이 말을 은유적으로 사용하고 있다.

2) **You have a lot of activity in your brain** : Your[Their] mind is busy thinking of things. 당신의 마음이 여러 가지를 바쁘게 생각한다.

Writing Layout

 편집의 첫 부분에서 학생들에게 단수·복수를 구별하라고 지시하고 있다. 문단을 쓸 때 띄어쓰기에 대한 설명이다.

T: (Explaining about writing layout) After typing your title, **you have to enter, enter, enter** [1] or blank three letters, then begin to write your paragraph.

S1: Do you mean that there should be three space in between?

T: Three space? Uh-uh··· no. Actually, you can't say 'three space' **because three are not just one.** [2] Do you get it?

S1: Ah! Sorry.

T: You don't have to say sorry for that. A lot of people, even I, make mistakes, so don't be sorry, don't be ashamed. Okay? So, how shall we change it?

S1: Spaces! Because it isn't a singular word.

T: Yeah. You got right. Booyah! Good job.

Expressions used

1) **you have to enter, enter, enter** : The teacher is telling the students to hit the 'enter' key three times.
선생님은 학생들에게 'enter' 키를 3번 쳐야 한다고 말한다.

2) **because three are not just one** : The teacher is referring to the student's incorrect grammar usage. 'Three' is plural, so the student should have said, 'three spaces'. 선생님은 학생의 잘못된 문법 용법을 유의시키고 있다. 'Three'는 복수이므로, 학생은 'three spaces'라고 말했어야 했다.

Paragraph

 글쓰기를 위한 기초적인 준비 과정에 대해 설명하고 있다. 먼저 단락 (paragraph)의 개념에 대한 질문으로 담화를 시작하고 있다.

T: Hi, students! How's everything going? Today, we are going to learn how to write a paragraph. So, who knows a 'paragraph'?

S1: It is a part of an essay.

S2: It consists of sentences.

T: Yes, you guys really know what a paragraph is! Many people need help writing a paragraph. If you don't know how to write a paragraph, **it can be a difficult thing to do.**[1] Here is a way to make it easier. Let's see the papers I gave you. Before you start writing a paragraph, you need to decide two things; What are you writing about and what do you want to say?

Ss: Ah….

T: The purpose of any paragraph is to express an idea. Most paragraphs consist of a few related sentences.

S1: So we have to write sentences according to the topic?

T: Sure, you have to. **Sometimes it is needed but don't use them because you are not quite at the point of writing an essay.**[2]

S2: When are we writing an essay?

T: When you are ready with paragraphs. Hmm. Let me see. Where are we right now?

Paragraph

단락

Ss: Beginning of this page!

T: One popular way to create pre-writing ideas is to ask yourself questions about your subject. Here are some questions you might ask yourself; What do I know about this subject? How does this subject relate to me? What do I like or dislike about this subject? What words best describe it? Write only a word or phrase in response to each question.

Ss: We have to brainstorm?

T: Good. That's what you are going to do!

Tip Origin of 'Climax'
'Climax' comes from the Greek for 'ladder'. As you near the top of a series of rungs, you reach the climax. ('Climax'는 그리스 어의 '사다리'에서 유래한다. 사다리 가로대의 꼭대기에 올라감에 따라 당신은 클라이맥스에 도달한다.)

Expressions used

1) **it can be a difficult thing to do** : The teacher is referring to paragraph writing and how, in English writing, it can be difficult to write. 선생님은 단락쓰기와 영어쓰기에서는 그것을 쓰기가 어렵다는 것을 말하고 있다.

2) **you are not quite at the point of writing an essay** : The teacher is telling the students that they are not ready to write a full English essay. 선생님은 학생들이 아직 완전한 글을 쓸 준비가 되어 있지 않다고 말한다.

글쓰기의 기본적인 규정에 대한 설명이다. 문장 결합, 시제, 언어 사용, 구어와 문어의 구별 등을 순서대로 설명하고 있다.

A. Do not begin your sentences with and, but, so, because. Instead, combine two shorter sentences into one longer sentence, or use alternative words.

   ex : I like sports. And I like to listen to music.

   There are ways to fix this mistake.
   a. Combine both sentences into one longer sentence.
   → I like sports, and I like to listen to music.
   b. Use alternative words.
   → I like sports. Also, I like to listen to music.
B. Watch your verb tense!
   This is one of the biggest mistakes students make.[1] If you are talking about something in the past, be sure to use the past tense. If you are talking about something in the future, be sure to use the future tense, and so on. Also, be careful of using difficult verb tenses (have, had, etc.). You can usually use the three main verb tenses (past, present, future) with no problem.
C. Don't use informal English.
   This includes emotions(^^,^^;;, etc.). Don't use slang(wanna, gonna, etc.). Don't use swear words.

D. Don't speak to the reader.

Sometimes this is okay, but usually it is not. For example, don't write, 'What do you think about…' or 'Did you ever…' or 'You should…' Try not to use you in your writing.

E. There is no excuse for bad spelling. Always use a spell check when you are typing your papers.[2]

F. Watch your common mistakes and your Konglish.

G. Make sure you have strong topic sentences.

When I read the first sentence of every paragraph, I should know exactly what that paragraph is about.

H. Watch simple mistakes.

Many students make very simple mistakes because they don't check their work. For example, he have or 1 weeks. Always edit your paper after you finish writing. This is one of the biggest mistakes students make; **Always use a spell check when you are typing your papers.**

Expressions used

1) **This is one of the biggest mistakes students make**：This is the most common mistake students make.
   이것은 학생들이 하는 가장 일반적인 실수이다.

2) **Always use a spell check when you are typing your papers**：A spell check is essential when typing your letters.
   철자 확인은 글자를 타자 칠 때 매우 중요하다.

Steps of Writing

글쓰기의 단계

 다음은 글 쓰는 방법에 대하여 선생님이 학생들에게 나누어 준 유인물이다. 브레인스토밍, 글의 구조, 좋은 글을 쓰는 방법, 그리고 구체적인 예를 차례로 설명하고 있다.

A. Steps of Brainstorming

Step 1. Brainstorming

Brainstorming is a way to list all of your ideas. After you choose your topic, brainstorm or think of everything included in your topic. You don't have to use every idea in your paper, but it will help you think. You can just make a list. Don't worry about making sentences here.

Step 2. Outline

After you review your brainstorming list and choose what you exactly you want to write, create an outline, organizing your paper.

Step 3. 1st Draft

Any good paper should be written more than once. For the first draft, try to write without using your dictionary too much, and DO NOT write your paper in Korean first. Just write as best you can.

Step 4. Editing

After you finished checking your paper, write it again. You may edit it again and write it again as many times as you want.

Steps of Writing

글쓰기의 단계

B. Organization of a paragraph

Organization of a one-page paper—Usually, a one-page paper should have 3~4 paragraphs. The style is very similar and may seem boring at first, but it is the Western standard for writing.

- **1st paragraph: Introduction**—What are you going to write about?
- **2nd/3rd paragraph: Body**—This is the main part of the paper.
- **4th paragraph: Conclusion**—What did you just write about?

C. How to write a good paragraph

Step 1.

Remember that each paragraph needs a strong topic sentence. A topic sentence is the first sentence in the paragraph. Your topic sentence should introduce the information in that paragraph.

Step 2.

Each paragraph should have between 4 to 6 sentences.

Step 3.

Each paragraph should discuss only one main idea. If you want to introduce a new idea, start a new paragraph.

D. Example

This week for homework, you will have to write a one-page paper about your winter vacation.[1]
Let's give an example using my winter vacation.[2]

Step 1. Brainstorming—This is just a list of what I think of when I think about my winter vacation.

Malaysia, Singapore, Brunei, sister, food, Chinese shopping, Indian, palm trees, monkey, Batu Caves, Christmas, New Year, Kuala Lumpur, Penang, Melaka, mosques, temples, churches, walking, Hot, hotels, hostels, kind people, rickshaw, train, tired, wonderful, Petronas Towers, rivers, swimming, mosquitoes, fresh fruit, juice, Muslims, money

Step 2. Outline—This is the organization of my paper

A) Introduction paragraph
 1. Introduce each country

    2. Highlights of the trip

B) Body 2, 3, 4 paragraphs

    1. Singapore : a. sightseeing/b. people/c. clean

    2. Brunei : a. Muslim nation/b. kind people/c. the water village

    3. Malaysia : a. diversity/b. sightseeing highlights/c. Kuala Lumpur, Melaka, Penang

C) Conclusion—Summary of the trip

Step 3. Editing—After writing the paper, I will check it and write it again.

Expressions used

1) **This week for homework, you will have to write a one-page paper about your winter vacation**: We can say "You have to write about your winter vacation in one page". or "For (your) homework this week, you have to fill up one page about your winter vacation". "너의 겨울방학에 대해 한 페이지의 글을 써 와야 한다." 또는 "이번주 숙제로 너의 겨울방학에 대해 한 페이지의 글을 써 와야 한다."라고 말할 수 있다.

2) **Let's give an example using my winter vacation**: As an example/For an example, I'll talk about my winter vacation. 예를 들어 나의 겨울방학에 대해 이야기를 해보겠습니다.

Part 6

The most basic expression or form of encouragement is the teacher's positive body language; the encouraging and approachable manner, tone of voice and smile that say; "You can do it", "Hang in there", "You're trying hard", " You handle that well", "That's hard work, but …", "Give it your best shot", "I'm sure you'll make a responsible decision".

[William A. Rogers(2002), British Scholar]

격려를 하는 가장 기본적인 표현 양식은 선생님의 적극적인 신체 언어이다.: 용기를 주고 가까이하기 쉬운 태도, 다음과 같은 말을 미소 지으면서 하는 것.: "너는 할 수 있어 계속해", "열심이구나", "너는 그 일을 잘 할 수 있어", "어려운 일이었다. 그렇지만……", "최선을 다해서 해라", "책임 있는 결정을 내릴 것으로 확신한다."

Test and Homework
시험과 과제

학습내용

여기에서는 주어진 단어로 '문장 만들기', '글쓰기의 요령' 등에 대한 원어민의 설명을 살펴보겠다. 먼저 과제에 관련된 대화를 정리하고, 다음으로 시험 및 시험 문제 풀이에 대한 대화를 살펴보기로 한다.

평소 시험 문제로, 두 사람의 대화에서 밑줄 친 부분을 수정해야 한다.
원어민의 구체적인 설명은 해설(Expression used)에 수록하였다.

* Change the underlined words in the dialogue.

Minsu: Hey, Todd, <u>nice to meet you</u>!

Todd: You, too, Minsu. What have you been up to?

Minsu: <u>Nothing special.</u> I've been working a lot lately.

Todd: Are you still dating that same girl? What was her name?

Minsu: Oh, you mean Sumi? No, we <u>split apart</u> 2 months ago. She was always flirting with other guys.

Todd: Aww, I'm sorry. That really sucks. <u>Do you want to have a blind date?</u>

Minsu: I really hate blind dates because you never know what to expect. But <u>I really need to make a girlfriend soon.</u>

Todd: Okay, <u>how about I plan a meeting with my sister?</u> She's about your age and she's also single.

Minsu: Can you describe her to me? I really want to <u>know her mind.</u>

Todd: Well, she's very athletic and <u>she likes to take a picture.</u>

Minsu: She sounds interesting. <u>Let's an appointment for this weekend.</u>

Todd: Let's meet at my house so <u>come to there</u> at Saturday.

Tip Zebra's stripes

A zebra's stripes make them stand out in a zoo, but in their natural habitat, the grasslands of Africa, the stripes act as camouflage and help conceal them from predators.
(얼룩말의 줄무늬는 동물원에서는 눈에 두드러집니다. 그러나 자연의 거주지, 아프리카의 초원에서는 줄무늬가 위장으로서의 역할을 하며, 육식 동물로부터 숨겨줍니다.)

Expressions used

1) **Minsu : Hey, Todd, <u>nice to meet you</u>!**
Note : When you meet someone for the first time you can say 'Nice to meet you'. However, after that you should say 'Nice to see again / Nice seeing you again'.
당신이 누군가를 처음 만났을 때 'Nice to meet you'를 사용한다. 하지만 그 다음에는 'Nice to see again / Nice seeing you again'과 같은 표현을 사용한다.

2) **Todd : You, too, Minsu. What have you been up to?**
Note : 'What have you been up to?' : What kinds of things have you been doing since I last saw you? 'What have you been up to?' asks which activities you have been doing, not the importance of an activity.
지난번 만난 뒤에 무엇을 했느냐? 'What have you been up to?'는 어떤 일을 했느냐를 묻고 있으며, 그 행위의 중요성을 묻는 것은 아니다.

3) **Minsu : <u>Nothing special</u>. I've been working a lot lately.**
Note : We usually say 'Nothing much / Not much'. 'Nothing special' means that what you have done is not important : e.g. My vacation was boring. I didn't do anything special.
'별일 없어'라는 의미로 'Nothing special'이라 하지 않고, 보통 'Nothing much / Not much'라고 한다. 'Nothing special'은 당신이 한 일이 중요한 일이 아니었다는 의미이다. 예. 방학은 지루했어. 특별히 한 일은 없었어.

4) **Todd : Are you still dating that same girl? What was her name?**
Note : Are you seeing / Are you still with the same girl? What was her name again? I forgot it. 여전히 같은 여자를 사귀니? 이름이 뭐였지? 잊어버렸어.

Expressions used

5) Minsu : Oh, you mean Sumi? No, we <u>split apart</u> 2 months ago.
She was always flirting with other guys.
Note: We say 'we broke up / split up' or 'I broke up / split up with her'. 'split up' means to be no longer together or to be divided: e.g. Split up the class into boys and girls.
'헤어지다'의 의미로는 주로 'we broke up / split up' 또는 'I broke up / split up with her' 라고 한다. 'split up'은 주로 '함께 있지 않다, 나누다'라는 의미로 사용된다.

6) Todd : Aww, I'm sorry. That really sucks. <u>Do you want to have a blind date</u>?
Note : Do you want me to set you up with someone / some girl?
'suck' means 'terrible' and is used to express disappointment at a situation : e.g. It sucks that I have so much homework.
'소개시켜 줄까?'라는 의미로는 'Do you want me to set you up with someone / some girl?'라고 표현한다. 'Suck'은 '아주 싫은, 매우 불만족한'이라는 의미로 어떤 상황에 대한 실망을 표현하기 위해 사용된다.

7) Minsu : I really hate blind dates because you never know what to expect. But <u>I really need to make a girlfriend soon</u>.
Note : I really need to find a girlfriend soon.
곧 여자친구를 찾고 싶다.

8) Todd : Okay, <u>how about I plan a meeting with my sister</u>? She's about your age and she's also single.
Note : How about setting up a date with my sister?
'How about' means another option for you to consider. It's asking for your option about something. It's the same as 'What about' : e.g. How about sushi tonight? Does that sound good?
'How about'는 당신의 또 다른 선택을 의미한다. 그것은 당신의 선택을 묻고 있는 것이다. 'What about'라고 할 수도 있다. : 생선회 어때? 좋지 않니?

Expressions used

9) Minsu : Can you describe her to me? I really want to <u>know her mind</u>.

   Note: You should say 'I really want to know how she thinks', 'I really want to get to know her' or 'I really want to find out what she's like'. 다음과 같이 바꾸어 말해야 한다. 'I really want to know how she thinks.' 'I really want to get to know her.' 'I really want to find out what she's like.'

10) Todd : Well, she's very athletic and <u>she likes to take a picture</u>.

   Note: She likes taking [to take] pictures. 'athletic' means she enjoys sports and the outdoors : e.g. She is very athletic because she is always running, exercising and hiking.

   그녀는 사진 찍는 것을 좋아한다. 'athletic'은 운동과 실외 활동을 즐기는 것을 의미한다. : 그녀는 달리기, 실내 운동, 등산을 즐기기 때문에 매우 건강하다.

11) Minsu : She sounds interesting. Let's an appointment for this weekend.

   Note : You should say 'Let's meet up this weekend'. or 'I want to meet her this weekend'. 'Let's meet up this weekend'. 또는 'I want to meet her this weekend'라고 표현해야 한다.

12) Todd : Let's meet at my house so come to there at Saturday.

   Note : You should say 'Come over on Saturday' or 'Let's (all) meet at my house on Sat'.

   'Come over on Saturday' or 'Let's (all) meet at my house on Sat'라고 표현해야 한다.

학생들이 영어 회화에서 흔히 실수하는 잘못된 문장을 수정하는 시험이다. 원어민 선생님이 평소 수업 중 학생들의 잘못된 표현을 모아 평소 시험을 통해 수정하였다.

* Correct the errors in the following sentences.

1. I really want to learning English to high skill level.
2. I want to making a relationship with wide people all over the world.
3. I think that I should break out with my girlfriend.
4. If I have a big stress I can't sleep very well. Homework gives me a big stress.
5. Kyeongbok Gung was palace for Joseon dynasty in Korea history.
6. Bibimbap is very healthful food so I recommend that to you.
7. If someone addicted to gambling, someone lose one's everything.
8. I want to study in Korea and I really envy a Korean culture.
9. First you should go to Jeju. Because it is very beautiful island and has many fresh and clean scenery.
10. People will lose many money when they do gambling so don't that.
11. I think the best food style is France style.
12. Sometimes people decide to suicide when he lost the

money.

13. You should eat daechang which is inside part of cow.

14. I want to go U.K. I really want to see the Europe. And, I like france wine.

15. I want to go Tai. Because there is much massage and beautiful woman.

16. I hope to go Swiss one day when I have money and time.

17. I want to meet the Britain people who are the most gentleman in the world.

18. And he eat drug and it is most dangerous.

19. There are many dangerous things but the most dangerous is shopper-holic.

20. After the war, Korea was splitted two nation.

Tip Time Measurement

Dividing the day into 24 hours, the hour into 60 minutes, and the minute into 60 seconds is an ancient system of time measurement but it did not come into general use until A.D. 1600. today, all cultures measure the day in the same way. However, in Kenya, seconds, minutes, and hours are the same but the day is split into two halves　from dawn until sunset, then sunset to sunrise. The two halves are more or less equal because the country is on the Equator. (날을 24시로, 시를 60분으로, 분을 60초로 나누는 것은 고대의 시간 측정 체계였지만, 1600년대 까지는 널리 사용되지 않았다. 그러나 케냐에서는 초, 분, 시간은 같지만 날은 양분된다. 그 나라가 적도에 있기 때문에 양분된 각각은 다소 비슷하다.)

Expressions used

아래의 수정에서 'Correct'는 학생들의 문장을 문법에 맞는 문장으로 수정한 것이며, 'Common'은 일반적으로 문어체에서 사용하는 표준 영어이고, 'Spoken'은 일상 생활의 대화에서 미국인들이 흔히 사용하는 표현이다. 다만 원어민마다 문어체와 일상적인 표현에 대한 판단 기준에서 상당한 차이가 있으므로 절대적 기준이라고 보기는 어렵다. 따라서 이를 고려하여 검토하면 도움이 될 것이다.

1) **I really want to learning English to high skill level.**
   → 'to'부정사와 전치사의 사용에 오류가 있다.

   Correct〉 I really want to learn English at a high skill level.

   Common〉 I really want to learn advanced English.

   Spoken〉 I really want to speak better English.

2) **I want to making a relationship with wide people all over the world.**
   → 'relationship'은 지나치게 격식적(too formal)이므로 일상적인 표현으로는 부적절하다. 또한 성적인 의미를 함축할 우려도 있다.

   Correct〉 I want to make relationships with people from all over the world.

   Common〉 I want to make friends with people from all over the world.

   Spoken〉 I want to meet people from around the world.

3) **I think that I should break out with my girlfriend.**
   → 'break out'(탈출하다, [여드름이]나다)와 'break up with'(관계를 끊다)를 구별해야 한다.

   Correct〉 I think I should break up with my girlfriend.

   Common〉 I think I should split up with my girlfriend.

   Spoken〉 I'm going to leave my girlfriend.

   cf.'Break out' means 'escape' or 'develop' a skin affliction such as rash or acne:e.g. The prisoner broke out from jail using a stolen key./I broke out with acne this morning. 'Break out'는 '탈출하다' 또는 '뾰루지와 발진 같은 피부병이 나다'는 의미이다.:예. 그 죄수는 훔친 열쇠를 사용해서 감옥에서 탈출했다./오늘 아침 얼굴에 발진이 생겼다.

4) **If I have a big stress I can't sleep very well. Homework gives me a big stress.**

Expressions used

→ 'stress'를 수식하는 형용사에 대한 오류이다.

Correct〉 If I have a lot of stress I can't sleep very well. Homework gives me a lot of stress.

Common〉 If I am under heavy stress I can't get sound sleep.[I can't get/have a good night's sleep/rest] Homework lays[puts] heavy stress on me.

Spoken〉 Homework stresses me out so much, I can't sleep well.

5) **Kyeongbok Gung was palace for Joseon dynasty in Korea history.**

→ 관사의 사용에 대한 오류이다.

Correct〉 Kyeongbok Gung was a palace for the Joseon dynasty in Korean history.

Common〉 Kyeongbok Gung was the palace of the Joseon dynasty in Korea.

Spoken〉 Kyeongbok palace was from the Joseon Dynasty.

6) **Bibimbap is very healthful food so I recommend that to you.**

→ 관사와 형용사의 구별에 관한 것이다. 명사 대용어로는 'that'이 아니라 'it'을 사용해야 한다.

Correct〉 Bibimbap is a very healthful/healthy food, so I recommend it to you.

Common〉 In the Korean diet, Bibimbap is a very healthy food, so you should try it.

Spoken〉 Korean Bibimbap is really healthy. I think you should order it [should try it].

cf. 'Healthy' is more common than 'healthful'. 'Healthy'가 'healthful' 보다 일반적으로 사용된다.

7) **If someone addicted to gambling, someone lose one's everything.**

→ 수동태와 능동태의 구별에 대한 오류이다. 'someone'은 구어체에서 대용어로 'they'를 흔히 사용한다.

Correct〉 If someone is addicted to gambling, they will/could lose everything.

Common〉 If you are indulged in gambling, you will be broke in a moment.

Spoken〉 If you are hooked on gambling, you'll probably lose everything [go bankrupt, lose it all]

8) **I want to study in Korea and I really envy a Korean culture.**

Expressions used

→ 관사 사용의 오류이다.

Correct〉 I want to study in Korea and I really envy the Korean culture.

Common〉 I'd like to study in Korea because I'm really interested in (the) Korean culture.

Spoken〉 I want to study in Korea because I'm really into Korean culture.

9) **First you should go to Jeju. Because it is very beautiful island and has many fresh and clean scenery.**

→ 부사절에 대한 오류이다.

Correct〉 First, you should go to Jeju island because it is a very beautiful island and has beautiful scenery.

Common〉 First you should go to Jeju-do because the island is very beautiful and has many beautiful places.

Spoken〉 You should go to Jeju-do. It's really tropical and the beaches are nice.

cf. When you take a shower or a bath, you feel fresh and clean.

10) **People will lose many money when they do gambling so don't that.**

→ '도박하다'는 'do gambling'이 아니라 'gamble'이다.

Correct〉 People will lose a lot of money when they gamble, so don't do it.

Common〉 You will lose a lot of money if you gamble. Don't do it.

Spoken〉 Gambling will leave you broke. Gambling will make you bankrupt.

'leave broke'(빈털털이가 되다), 'make bankrupt'(파산하게 만들다)가 일반적인 어휘 결합 방식이다.

11) **I think the best food style is France style.**

→ 'Food'는 'style'이 아니다.

Correct〉 I think the best kind/type of food is French.

Common〉 I think French food is the best.

Spoken〉 French food rocks. [French food is really good.]

'rock'은 모든 점에서 좋을 때 사용한다. 그러나 어떤 여자를 보고 매우 외모가 멋있을 때에는 'She is hot.' (She is very beautiful)이라고 한다.

12) **Sometimes people decide to suicide when he lost the money.**
→ '자살하다'는 'commit suicide'로 표현한다.
Correct〉 Sometimes people decide to commit suicide when they lose money.
Common〉 Sometimes people often commit suicide because they lost their money.
Spoken〉 People sometimes commit suicide when they're bankrupt.

13) **You should eat daechang which is inside part of cow.**
→ 명확히 구분하면 동물의 창자는 'intestines', 내부 장기는 'innards'로 표현한다. 그러나 원어민들은 일상적으로 'innards'를 일상적으로 많이 사용한다.
Correct〉 You should eat daechang which is cow intestines [cow innards].
Common〉 You could try the Korean dish, daechang, which is made of cow innards.
Spoken〉 Do you want to try daechang? It's made from cow innards.

14) **I want to go U.K. I really want to see the Europe. And, I like france wine.**
→ 관사의 용법에 대한 오류이다.
Correct〉 I want to go to the U.K. I really want to see Europe. And, I like French wine.
Common〉 I'd like to travel to England. I'd like to look around Europe. Especially I'd like to taste French wine.
Spoken〉 I want to [wanna] to check out Europe, especially the U.K. Also, I want to drink French wine.

15) **I want to go Tai. Because there is much massage and beautiful woman.**
→ 우리말 전이에 따른 오류이다.
Correct〉 I want to go to Thailand because there are a lot of massages and beautiful women.
Common〉 I'd like to take a trip to Thailand because I can enjoy a massage and meet beautiful women.
Spoken〉 I really want to go to Thailand. It has great massages and beautiful girls.

16) **I hope to go Swiss one day when I have money and time.**

Expressions used

→ 우리말 전이에 따른 오류이다.

Correct〉 I hope to go to Switzerland one day[some day] when I have money and time.

Common〉 I'd like to take a trip to Switzerland when I afford it.

Spoken〉 I'd like to go to Switzerland when I can.

'Afford'는 경제적 의미를 함의하므로 친한 사이가 아닐 경우에는 사용하지 않는 것이 좋다.

17) **I want to meet the Britain people who are the most gentleman in the world.**

→ 불특정인에게는 정관사를 사용하지 않는다.

Correct〉 I want to meet British people who are the most gentlemanly in the world.

Common〉 I'd like to get to know British people because they are the most courteous in the world.

Spoken〉 I really want to meet British people. They're known for being so polite.

18) **And he eat drug and it is most dangerous.**

→ '동사+명사'로 구성된 관용어의 오류이다.

Correct〉 He takes/does drugs and it is the most dangerous thing to do.

Common〉 He takes/does drugs and it can cause a lot of trouble.

Spoken〉 He takes/does drugs. Taking [Doing] drugs can cause lots of problems.

19) **There are many dangerous things but the most dangerous is shopper-holic.**

→ 복합어의 오류이다.

Correct〉 There are many dangerous things but the most dangerous is being a shop-a-holic.

Common〉 There are many dangerous/serious things in life [in the world] but a shopper-a-holic is the worst.

Spoken〉 A shop-a-holic is a dangerous person. They'll blow [spend] all of their money on clothes.

20) **After the war, Korea was splitted two nation.**

→ 전치사의 탈락에 의한 오류이다.

Expressions used

Correct〉 After the war, Korea was split into two nations.

Common〉 After the civil war, Korea was divided into two countries.

Spoken〉 Korea was divided in half [two] after the war.

다음 자료는 구두점(punctuation)의 극단적인 사용에 대한 예문으로, 동일한 내용이 구두점에 의해 상반되는 의미를 지닐 수 있다는 점을 강조하기 위한 것이다. 구두점에 관한 학습에 유용한 자료로 이용할 수 있다. 원래 Lynne Truss(2003)의 예문으로 원어민의 해설을 첨가하였다.

* **Explain the meaning difference between the following two paragraphs.**

Dear Minsu

I want a man **who knows what love is all about.**[1] You are generous, kind, thoughtful. People who are not like you admit to being useless and inferior. **You have ruined me for other men.**[2] I yearn for you. **I have no feelings whatsoever when we're apart.**[3] I can be forever happy — will you let me be yours?

From Sunhi

해석: 나는 사랑의 의미를 아는 사람을 원합니다. 당신은 관대하고, 친절하고, 사려 깊습니다. 당신과 같지 않은 사람은 쓸모없고 열등한 인간입니다. 나는 당신 이외에는 어떤 사람도 생각하지 않습니다. 나는 당신을 그리워합니다. 우리가 떨어져 있으면 당신 외에 아무 생각이 없습니다. 나는 영원히 행복할 수 있습니다. — 당신의 아내가 되게 해 주세요.

....

Dear Minsu,

I want a man who knows what love is. All about you are generous, kind, thoughtful people **who are not like you.**[4] Admit

to being useless and inferior. You have ruined me. For other men I yearn! For you I have no feelings whatsoever. When we're apart I can be forever happy. **Will you let me be?**[5]
Yours,

From Sunhi

해석: 나는 사랑이 무엇인지 아는 사람을 원합니다. 당신 주위의 모든 사람은 관대하고, 친절하고, 사려 깊은 사람들이며, 당신과는 다릅니다. 쓸모없고 열등한 것을 인정하세요. 당신은 나를 망쳤습니다. 나는 다른 사람을 그리워합니다. 당신에 대해서는 아무런 관심이 없습니다. 우리가 헤어지면 나는 영원히 행복할 수 있습니다. 나를 내버려 두세요.

Expressions used

1) **who knows what love is all about**: who know the meaning of love 사랑의 의미를 아는

2) **You have ruined me for other men**: I can't think of being with anyone except you. 당신 이외의 다른 사람과 함께 있는 것을 생각할 수 없습니다.

3) **I have no feelings whatsoever when we're apart**: That means 'I can't think about anything else but you'. However that sentence usually implies negative meaning: I don't care about you any more. You mean nothing to me.
'나는 당신 이외에는 아무 생각도 없습니다'라는 뜻이다. 그러나 대체로 이 문장은 오히려 '너에 대해 신경쓰지 않는다. 너는 나에게 중요하지 않다'는 부정적 의미로 해석된다.

4) **who are not like you**: who are different from you 당신과는 다른

5) **Will you let me be?**: Will you leave me alone? Get away from me. 내게서 떠나주세요.

아래의 관용어를 이용하여 문장을 만드는 시험이다. 관용어를 활용하여 다양한 영어 능력 평가를 할 수 있다는 것을 보여주고 있다.

1. In a sentence, describe an experience where you were on the edge of your seat.

2. In a sentence, describe the last occasion when you took someone up on something.

3. Use the idiom, 'buckle down', in a sentence so that the meaning of the idiom is clearly understood.

4. Have you or anyone you know ever had to live from hand to mouth? Explain the circumstances using the idiom in a sentence.

5. Using the idiom, 'dead wrong' in a sentence, give an example of a time when you felt that someone was dead wrong.

6. Have you ever had a teacher who really piled on the work? Use the idiom in a sentence to explain the situation.

7. How can a person move up the ladder in Korea? Use the idiom in a sentence to explain.

8. In a sentence, use the idiom, 'pass up' and describe the last time you had to pass up an opportunity.

9. In a sentence, give the meaning of 'get something of one's chest'.

10. Is there anything you are fed up with right now? Explain, using the idiom in a sentence.

11. Looking back on your past, have you ever done anything wrong? Use the idiom, 'in hindsight', in a sentence to explain what it is you think you did wrong.

12. Have you ever had to swallow your pride? Use the idiom in a sentence and explain the circumstances.

13. What are three things that bore you to death? Explain in one complete sentence.

14. Using the idiom, 'stick it out', and explain in one sentence a situation where you hated doing something but you stuck it out to the end.

15. Have you ever had a teacher spark your interest in a subject you thought was boring or difficult? Explain the circumstances using the idiom in a sentence.

Tip Fewer vs Less
'Fewer' is the comparative form of 'few' and is used with plural nouns to mean 'not as many': There were fewer people in the department today. Use 'less' with singular nouns: We had less time today. ('Fewer'는 'few'의 비교급으로 복수명사와 함께 사용되며, '그만큼 많지 않은'의 의미로 사용된다. : 오늘 백화점에는 평소보다 사람이 더 적었다. 'less'는 단수명사와 함께 사용된다. : 우리는 오늘 시간이 많지 않았다.)

원어민이 학생들에게 시험 전에 배포해 준 회화 시험(conversation questions)과 말하기 평가 시험(oral assessment questions)에 대한 문제이다. 유인물을 제출한 다음 마지막으로 회화 문제에서 2개, 말하기 평가 문제에서는 1개를 출제할 예정이며, 시간은 2분 정도 소요될 것이라고 설명하고 있다.

Conversation Questions : (회화 시험)

1. What are some ways that students can take the initiative to speak with native speakers of English?

2. In Korean culture, what types of behavior are looked down on?

3. What is something that you only do once in a blue moon? Why?

4. Is there a minimum wage in Korea? Is it enough for people to live on?

5. What technological advancement has affected your life the most? Why?

6. What's your favorite holiday or festival? Why?

7. What's the most interesting holiday or festival in Korea?

8. Talk about Korean marriage customs.

9. How has life at the Naval Academy changed over the years?

10. Talk about your skills and job preferences.

11. What kind of career or job would you be good at? Why?

Oral Assessment Questions : (말하기 평가 시험)

1. Using an infinitive or gerund, describe the use or purpose of a satellite, DNA fingerprinting, a MP3 player, an industrial robot, or the World Wide Web.

2. Using an infinitive complement, give advice on how to use a digital camera, a microwave oven, a cellular phone, a MP3 player, or in-line skates.

3. In a sentence, give the definition of the verb unplug.

4. In a sentence, give the definition of psychotherapist.

5. Using a relative clause of time, give some information about August 15th, the Okpo Festival, spring, or Chuseok.

6. Using an adverbial clause of time, explain what happens to a Korean before he gets married, at a Korean wedding ceremony, to a Korean couple when they return from their honeymoon, or when they get engaged.

7. In a sentence, give the definition of American Valentine's Day, fireworks, bridal shower, newlywed, or wedding anniversary.

8. In a sentence, describe student life at the Naval Academy nowadays.

9. In a sentence, describe what student life at the Naval

Academy might be like in twenty years.

10. Using a conditional sentence with an if clause, describe what might happen if you start smoking, if you leave the Naval Academy to go to another university, if you win the lottery, if you don't get married, if Korea wins the World Cup of soccer in 2006, if there is a revolution in North Korea, or if you have more free time.

11. Using an affirmative statement with a gerund, what is something that you like doing?/what is something you are good at?/what is something you are interested in?

12. Using a negative statement with a gerund, what is something you hate doing, you don't mind doing, or you are not good at?

13. Using a clause with because, explain why you would be a good naval office, make a good husband [wife], make a good father [mother], or make a good teacher.

14. In a sentence, give the definitions of punctual, impatient, and efficient.

....

T: Your speaking test will consist of 10 randomly chosen questions from this list. One question from the oral assessment questions will be chosen, as well as two of the conversation questions. For the questions chosen from the oral assessment questions **your answer must be one sentence answers.**[1] The answer must be a complete sentence, not a part of a sentence or incomplete sentence. For the conversation questions, **you and I will engage in a short conversation on the two topics that are randomly chosen.**[2] The conversations will be approximately 2 minutes each.

Expressions used

1) **your answer must be one sentence answers** : This is an instruction to the students that their answers must be no longer than one sentence.
이것은 학생들의 답이 한 문장을 넘지 않아야 한다는 지시다.

2) **you and I will engage in a short conversation on the two topics that are randomly chosen** : 'Engage' in a conversation means to have a conversation. So, the teacher is telling the students that they will have a conversation on two randomly chosen topics.
회화에 '참여한다(engage)'는 말은 회화를 한다는 것이나. 따라서 선생님은 학생들에게 그들이 마음대로 선택한 화제를 가지고 회화를 할 것이다라고 말하고 있다.

수업 전 읽기 예습을 했는지 확인하고 있다. 학생들이 읽기 예습 숙제를 안 했기 때문에 선생님이 다시 기사를 5분만에 읽으라고 지시한다.

T: OK, guys! Next page. Did you read this article?

Ss: ….

T: Oh, come on!¹⁾

S1: What was that? ²⁾

T: You don't know? Remember you had homework? OK. Why don't you take five minutes to read this article. OK? Go ahead!

(Students do what they are told.)

Tip Origin of 'Alphabet'
The word 'alphabet' comes from the first two letters of the Greek alphabet, 'alpha' and 'beta'.
('Alphabet'이라는 단어는 그리스 어 알파벳의 첫 두 지인 '알파'와 '베타'로부터 유래되있다.)

Expressions used

1) **Oh, come on!**: The teacher is a little shocked that the students didn't read the article. Slightly angry.
학생들이 그 내용을 읽지 않은 것에 선생님이 약간 충격을 받았다. 약간 기분이 상했다.

2) **What was that?**: The student is asking, 'What article were we supposed to read?' '어느 내용을 읽게 되어 있습니까'라고 학생이 묻고 있다.

Homework

 요약 숙제가 어렵다는 학생에게 수업 중 주의를 기울이지 않았기 때문이라고 지적하고 있다.

T: Let's get started. Was the homework easy?

S1: No, it was difficult.

T: Really? What was so difficult?

S1: Writing the summary of the reading material.

T: What? **We did the summary in class!**[1] I gave you this for homework to find out if you paid attention in class.

S1: Really? I did not know we did this in class.

T: How many times did I say 'Pay attention!' in class?

S1: I'm sorry, John. I will pay attention to what we do in class.

T: In this case, you will have to write the summary and your rough draft by next Wednesday. Now, homework; Choose one innovation. **I don't care about what machines.**[2] What are the pros and cons on the machine? Do you know pros and cons?

Ss: No.

T: Pros means positive things and cons the negative things. And preview Unit 3, Interchange. Just look through it and vocabulary. Good job today. Have a good week.

suck

The slang 'suck' means to be contemptible or very unsatisfying because of its low quality:
The movie is a flop because it sucks. (속어인 'suck' 저질이다)는 질이 나빠서 경멸스럽거나 만족스럽지
못하다는 뜻이다.: 그 영화는 저질이기 때문에 실패작이다.)

Expressions used

1) **We did the summary in class!** : The teacher is speaking on the
fact that a student had difficulty writing a summary on some
teaching material. The teacher is slightly angry because the sum—
mary was done together in the previous class.
선생님은 학생이 학습 자료를 요약하는 데 어려움을 가졌다는 사실을 언급하고 있다. 선
생님은 이전 시간에 함께 요약을 했기 때문에 다소 기분이 언짢다.

2) **I don't care about what machines** : The teacher is telling the
students that he/she does not care what machines (innovations)
the students choose to write about.
선생님은 학생이 어떤 기기에 대해 기술하든 개의치 않는다고 말하고 있다.

Project

 주어진 과제에 대한 확인을 마친 뒤, 유인물을 나누어 주고 다음 시간에 시험을 친다고 예고하는 담화이다. 이때 알렉스가 어느 정도 쓸 것인가 선생님에게 묻고 있다.

T: What else this week? Now, I want to collect the projects this week.

Ss: Nobody.

T: Nobody?

Alexander: Somebody. [1] (He gives his homework.)

Elly: Me too. (She hands in her homework.)

　　(Some student at the corner laughs all of sudden.)

T: What's happening over there? Anything wrong?

Nippy: He.

Terry: She sent me an e-mail first, but she didn't answer because Nippy stole my penpal!

Ss: (laugh)

T: Does that mean Nippy is more popular to girls than Terry?

Ss: Haha··· yeah···!

Terry: No! Only that email girl special!

Nippy: No, I'm more handsome.

Ss: No. (laugh).

T: So, **Elly and Alexander are the only ones to finish?** [2] Elly, how long did it take?

Elly: 4 days.

T: Alexander?

Alexander: 2 days.

T: Only 2 days? Alex, do you have any advice for the students who didn't finish?

Alex: You have to get up early. So **your suggestion is to take time.** [3]

T: Elly, how about you?

Elly: The same.

T: Then did anybody not start the project? Any questions about the project? Anything that you're having problems with? Hand in your project this class next week···. Now, I'll hand out a paper. Study it. There will be a quiz on it.

Alex: What is the boundary of the quiz? [4]

T: What do you mean by 'boundary'?

Alex: This quiz sheet how much?

T: The quiz will be only the front page of this sheet. [5]

Project

과제

Expressions used

1) **Somebody**: I think the student is saying that at least one person completed the homework assignment. However, the English is poor, so I'm not sure. 적어도 한 사람은 숙제를 했다고 학생이 말하고 있다. 그러나 영어가 너무 서툴러서 확신하기가 어렵다.

2) **Elly and Alexander are the only ones to finish?**: The teacher is commenting on the fact that only these two students completed the assignment. 선생님은 단지 이 두 학생이 숙제를 했다는 사실을 언급하고 있다.

3) **your suggestion is to take time**: The student is using poor English in an attempt to advise other students to take their time when doing an assignment because it is difficult. He should say 'You should devote more time to your homework' or 'I suggest that you should spend a lot of time doing your homework'.
학생은 서툰 영어로 다른 학생들에게 숙제가 어렵기 때문에 그것을 할 때에는 시간이 걸린다고 충고하려고 한다. 그는 '숙제에 더 많은 시간을 투자해야 한다' 또는 '숙제를 하는 데 많은 시간을 보내야 한다'고 말했어야 한다.

4) **What is the boundary of the quiz?**: The student is using poor English to ask how much space on the paper is needed to complete the quiz answers. 학생들이 서툰 영어로 퀴즈에 답을 쓰기 위해서 얼마나 많은 양이 필요한가를 묻고 있다.

5) **The quiz will be only the front page of this sheet**: The teacher's response to the question is that only one side of one sheet of paper will be necessary to complete the quiz.
그 질문에 대해 선생님은 퀴즈에 답하는 데 단지 종이의 한 면만 필요하다고 대답한다.

Pop Quiz

즉석 시험

 즉석 시험 문제를 배포하고 시험 시간을 10분으로 정했다. 학생들이 5분 더 연장하기를 요구하지만 선생님은 정확히 시간을 지킨다.

T: Attention everyone. **We're going to take a pop quiz today!** [1]

Ss: A pop quiz?!? No way!!!

T: Will you pass these around?

S1: Sure.

T: And it starts now! You'll have 10 minutes.

(In 10 minutes) Have you all finished?

S2: Not yet! 5 more minutes please.

T: Time's up! Let's check how well you did.

S2: It's not fair!

T: Too bad. We're going to take a 10 minute break.

Tip Usage of 'Comma'

We usually write a comma in places where we would make a slight pause if we were speaking the words. A comma can also show that one part of a sentence is separate: When you leave, please shut the door. (우리가 말할 때 잠깐 멈추는 위치에 '쉼표'를 쓴다. '쉼표'는 문장의 한 부분이 분리된 것을 나타낼 수도 있다.: 나갈 때, 문 닫으세요.)

Expressions used

1) **We're going to take a pop quiz today!** : A 'pop' quiz is an unannounced, surprise quiz. 즉석 시험은 예고 없이 불시에 치는 시험이다.

기말 시험 범위에 대한 설명문이다. 오류 문제가 많이 출제될 것이며, 교과 참여 비중도 높다는 점을 알리고 있다.

T: For just a moment, I want to talk about our finals today. Are you listening? Terry, what's the problem? Why are we so talkative today?

Terry: Nothing.

T: Your final exam will be chapters 1 and 2 from this book, and chapters 1, 2 and 3 from that book. And **a big part will be the common mistakes.**[1] It's the same kind of questions as the last time. **However, class participation is the most important in class, as much as the finals.**[2]

Tip Colors of the spectrum

Remember the order of the colors of the spectrum red, orange, yellow, green, blue, indigo, violet by using a mnemonic (a word or sentence made up of the first letter of each word.): 'Richard of York gave battle in vain' or 'Roy G. Biv'. (스펙트럼의 색깔의 순서[빨주노초파남보]를 연상법[각 단어의 첫 번째 문자로 구성된 단어나 문장]을 사용하여 기억하세요.: 요크 지역의 리차드가 허망하게 전쟁에 졌다. 로이 G.비브.)

Expressions used

1) **a big part will be the common mistakes**:a large part of the test will have questions from the common mistakes [will focus on common mistakes].
상당 부분의 시험이 일반적 오류에 대한 시험이다[일반적 오류에 중점을 둘 것이다].

2) **However, class participation is the most important in class, as much as the finals**:However, class participation is just as important as finals and is worth just as much.
그러나 수업 참여 활동이 기말고사만큼 중요하고 가치가 있다.

기말고사에 출제되는 교과서의 시험 범위에 대해 설명하고 있다. 마지막에는 구체적인 문항 수와 관용구가 출제되는 단원에 대해 언급하고 있다.

T: For those juniors, you guys need to go over Units 1 to 4 in 'All Clear' and 7 to 10 in 'New Interchange'. Remember! **This final test will cover everything that you have been studying!** [1]

Ss: Ah. Come on!

T: No! I'm not joking with you now! This test is going to be difficult if you do not study. OK?

S1: John!

T: Yes, please.

S1: Can you give us some hints?

T: Well, as I just said the final test includes every chapter. So, basically you should study on your own and come to see me whenever you have a question. OK? Or else go to see the T.A.s.

S2: Is that all you can say?

T: **Well, why don't I say this···** [2] you should write this down.

Ss: (Take their notes out.)

T: You will have a total of 50 questions. And you have 25 idiom questions out of 50 questions. The most idiom questions should come from units 3 and 4. But this does not mean that you do not have to study Units 1 and 2. OK?

Ss: ···.

T: OK! Guys! Do you have any other questions? Remember, guys, today is the last Standard of Evaluation class before the test day. No questions? Are you guys all ready?

Ss: Yes!

T: Cool! Then, good luck on your test! Good bye!

Tip Suffixes '-ful' vs '-less'

The suffix '-ful' means full of. It is usually spelled with just one 'l'. 'Careful' means 'full of care or taking care'. The suffix '-less' means without, e.g. 'careless'. (어미 '-ful'은 '가득 찬'을 의미한다. 그것은 대개 하나의 'l'만 쓴다. 'Careful'은 관심이나 주의를 많이 기울이는 것을 의미한다. 어미, '-less'는 없다는 의미이다. 예, '주의없는')

Expressions used

1) **This final test will cover everything that you have been studying!**: The teacher is telling the students that everything from the entire semester will be on the final exam.
선생님은 학생들에게 전 학기에 배운 모든 것이 기말시험에 나올 것이라고 말한다.

2) **Well, why don't I say this**: The teacher will not tell the students exactly what is on the test, but he/she is telling the students how many questions will be on the test and what types of questions they will be. 선생님은 학생들에게 시험에 정확히 무엇이 출제될 것인지는 말하지 않을 것이다. 그러나 학생들에게 시험이 몇 문제나 출제되며, 어떤 유형이 출제될 것인지는 말할 것이다.

After Exam

 중간고사로 10과목을 치른 뒤, 기계공학과 학생들을 대상으로 각 과목에 대해 선생님과 잡담을 나누고 있다. 학생들은 선택 과목 1과목 이외는 모두 공통이라고 말하고 있다.

T: How were the midterm exams last week?

S1: In fact, **we had to study about 10 subjects.**

T: What class?

S1: Engineering.

T: All of you have the same class schedule?

S2: Except just one class. **Elective is different.** [2]

T: You, you and you take Literature?

Ss: Yes.

T: And the rest of you have Professor Hwang?

Ss: Yes.

T: So what was the most difficult subject?

S2: Engineering.

S3: Also American Culture.

S4: I'm very weak. I'm very poor of writing in Korean.

T: Your writing is not good? But you are a good English writer.

S4: Oh, no, no. Thank you, thank you. **I was not a literature class.** [3] I was a math student.

T: So you were stronger at science and at math.

S4: Yes. So my Korean literature is more weaker.

T: Not more weaker···

S4: More··· more weak. 아니 just weaker.

T: Yes, good job. I hope you did well on the exam.

S4: Thank you, Nina.

T: How about the easiest exam?

S5: No.

S3: There were no easy exams.

T: OK, so what kind of things do you learn in American culture?

S1: Lifestyle, characteristics, history.

S2: We are learning a lot of things.

T: Are they new things?

S1: Yes, yes, they are new and interesting.

S4: **For me boring, sorry, haha.** [4)]

T: That's OK, if my culture is boring. Good to be honest. You said that you're learning history in that class. What did you learn?

S1: The independence.

S2: How the Protestants looked a soften view on military because of President Kennedy.

T: So what did you write for the exam?

S3: Two things.

S5: About the 400, 500 war.

T: Do you remember any of the questions?

S2: Yes, I remember.

T: Give me any.

S3: Which is the difference between the right brained and the left brained?

T: So what is the difference?

S2: Right brain is emotional, and left brain is logical.

T: Who's emotional here?

(One student raises hand.)

S6: I am very emotional.

Ss: Hahahaha.

S2: I heard that **most of the right brained person is left handed.** [5)]

S6: Oh, I am left handed.

Ss: Ah, haha.

T: What other questions?

S3: Big city and small town, which is better?

T: So these were just opinion questions, no right or wrong answers.

S1: Yeah, they were just debates.

S2: One was explaining about their American culture and their religion. Second one was about history, and third was American characteristics.

T: Wow, this is very interesting for me.

S1: We can divide it into three.

S7: One is race.

S3: Second one is social.

T: And the final one?

S7: Last one is lifestyle.

T: Lifestyle?

S6: Um⋯ maybe different characteristics, or you know.

T: I heard from Commander Lee that there will be a person coming to tell you about military culture.

S3: Yes, they came, and another guy told us about the military and their life story.

T: Could you understand his thinking?

S2: Yes, but not all of it.

S1: I told him we understand.

T: That's very brave of you.

S1: Haha, thank you. One thing that was very interesting was that they were in England when we were there.

T: Wow, it's a small world.

S1: Yeah⋯ but we didn't meet him.

Tip Spelling of compound words

English spelling does not allow tripes of the same letter, so where a compound word contains three of the same letters consecutively a hyphen is inserted, as in bell-like and cross-section. (영어 철자는 같은 문자가 3개 붙은 것을 허용하지 않는다. 따라서 같은 문자 3개를 연속적으로 포함하는 복합어는 하이픈을 첨가한다.)

Expressions used

1) **we had to study about 10 subjects** : The student is trying to tell the teacher how many subject tests the students had to study for. 학생이 선생님에게 학생들이 몇 과목에 대해 공부를 해야 하는지 말하고 있다.

2) **Elective is different** : Poor English. The student is trying to explain that the elective course tests are done differently than the required tests. 서툰 영어. 학생은 선택과정 시험은 필수시험보다 다르게 치러진다는 것을 설명하려고 한다.

3) **I was not a literature class** : Poor English. The student is trying to tell the teacher that he/she did not have a literature class. 서툰 영어. 그는 선생님에게 문학 수업을 받지 않았다고 말하고 있다.

4) **For me boring, sorry haha** : The student is telling the teacher that the class was boring. 학생이 선생님에게 그 수업은 지겹다고 말한다.

5) **most of the right brained person is left handed** : Poor English. The student is trying to say that people who are right brained (the right side of the brain is the dominant half) write and do other things with their left hands, i.e. they are left-handed. 서툰 영어. 학생은, 좌뇌 지배(뇌의 오른쪽이 지배하는 쪽) 사람들은 그들의 왼손으로 글을 쓰고 다른 것들을 하는, 즉 왼손잡이라는 것을 말하려고 한다.

Oral Test

구두 시험

주어진 질문을 파트너에게 한 뒤 답을 적고, 자신도 10개의 질문을 만들어 다시 파트너에게 질문하고 답을 적으라는 구두 시험이다.

T: Choose a partner and ask the following questions. **Make sure your partner answers in complete sentences.** [1] However, when you write your partner's answers, you do not have to write complete answers. After you finish asking all of the questions, **make 10 questions of your own** [2] and ask your partner.

Tip Seoul

Seoul has been an important settlement since 11th century. During the Korean War (1950~53) the city was badly damaged and changed hands four times. The city now has a population of more than 10 million. (서울은 11세기 이후 주요 거주지였다. 한국전쟁 동안 그 도시는 심하게 피괴되었으며, 4번이나 주인이 바뀌었다. 그 도시는 현재 인구가 천만 명이 넘는다.)

Expressions used

1) **Make sure your partner answers in complete sentences** : The teacher is telling the students that in this pair discussion activity, they must use complete English sentences. 선생님은 학생들에게 두 명씩 토의를 할 때 완전한 영어 문장을 사용해야 한다고 말하고 있다.

2) **make 10 questions of your own** : The teacher is telling the students that along with the questions the teacher provided, they must also ask ten of their own questions. 선생님은 그가 제시한 질문과 함께 학생들은 자신들이 스스로 10개의 질문을 물어야 한다고 말하고 있다.

Part 7

"What's one and one and one and one and one and one
and one and one and one?" "I don't know," said Alice.
"I lost count." "She can't do Addition." the Red Queen
interrupted.
[Lewis Carroll(1832~1898), English Author]

일 더하기, 일 더하기, 일 더하기, 일 더하기, 일 더하기, 일 더
하기, 일 더하기, 일 더하기, 일은 얼마? "몰라요. 세다가 잃어
버렸어요" 하고 엘리스가 말했다. 그러자 붉은 여왕은 끼어들
어 "그녀는 더하기를 못해요"라고 말했다.

Game
게임

학습내용 ——————
여기에서는 선택에 대한 게임,
어휘 만들기 게임, 몸짓 게임
을 차례대로 수록하였다. 게임
에는 일반적으로 준비 자료가
필요하며 그룹별로 활동이 이
루어져 수업이 산만해질 우려
가 있다.

Would You Rather?

매우 현실적으로 선택하기 어려운 두 가지 중 하나를 선택하여 인성을 이해하는 게임이다. 먼저 어휘 'rather'의 의미를 묻고 설명한 뒤에, 설문지에 있는 50개의 문항 중에 선택할 것을 지시하고 있다.

Nina: We're going to do an activity today. I hope it's fun for you. It's not exactly a game, but I thought it would be helpful to better your discussions. It's called 'Would you rather?' What does 'rather' mean?

S1: Or.

Nina: Either, or. **'Which do you prefer?'** [1] It has a list of 50 questions, and you have to choose one of the two. The problem is that they are very difficult questions. The two choices are either very good choices or very bad choices, but you must choose an answer for all questions and you must be honest when you answer. These questions will teach us about your true personality. All you need to do is circle the answer. Some of the vocabulary and the questions are difficult, so if you don't know the meaning, please ask me instead of just randomly circling an answer. (After handing out the questions.) OK, please write your names on these. For example, question 1 says, 'Would you rather be 1 meter taller or 1 meter shorter?' So just circle one answer that fits for you.

S1: (While students are laughing) I have a question. Where did you find these questions?

Nina: Some of them I made while some of them were from

Would You Rather?

오히려

the Internet.

S1: These are funny.

Nina: Yes, some are very thought-provoking. [2]

> **Tip** Making Crossword Puzzles
>
> Making your own crossword puzzles is a good way to practice spelling and helps you remember the meaning of words. Make a grid on a sheet of paper. Start with longish word either across or down the page. Then add words to it, using a letter from the original word. Write short definitions as clues. (혼자서 십자말풀이를 만드는 것은 철자를 만들고 단어의 의미를 기억하는 데 도움이 되는 좋은 방법입니다. 종이에 격자를 만드세요. 가로나 세로로 좀 긴 단어로 시작하세요. 그리고 거기에 원래의 단어의 철자를 이용하여 단어를 덧붙이세요. 짧은 정의를 힌트로 쓰세요.)

Expressions used

1) **Either, or. 'which do you prefer?'** : The teacher is explaining that 'rather' means you can do either A or B, which do you choose. 'rather'는 A 또는 B를 할 수 있으며, 당신은 어느 것을 택할 것인지를 의미한다.

2) **some are very thought-provoking** : 'Thought-provoking' means causes one to think seriously and deeply about one's response/ answer/belief. '깊게 생각해야 하는(thought-provoking)'은 대답 또는 믿음에 대해서 심각하고 깊이 생각해 보게 한다는 의미이다.

Gesture

 학생들이 몸짓의 의미를 알아내는 놀이이다. 먼저 그림 속의 몸짓의 의미를 알아 맞힌 다음, 각 팀별로 직접 몸짓를 취하고 다른 팀은 의미를 알아내도록 지시하고 있다.

T: Good morning, class!

Ss: (Tired) Good morning.

T: Why is everyone looking so tired?

S1: Yesterday's soccer game.

T: There was a soccer game yesterday?

S1: Yes. I watch yesterday night.

T: **You mean you watched it yesterday night?** [1] And so that's why you guys are so tired!

S2: They were very terrible! I couldn't sleep after the game!

T: In what area did they do bad?

S3: Everything. Offense, defense, shooting. And worstly⋯

T: Worst of all⋯

S3: Yes, worst of all they didn't even run.

T: Oh, maybe they were all tired too!

Ss: (heheheh⋯)

T: **They could be suffering from jet lag.** [2] Anyway, let's get to business. Turn to your books! Look at the gestures in page 56. What do you think the first picture means?

S4: That probably means, 'Are you crazy?'

T: What about #2?

S5: 'Come here.'

T: And #3?

Gesture

몸짓

S6: It probably mean 'Be quiet'.

T: What do you think #4 means?

S7: 'Be careful.'

T: Now comes the most exciting part of today's lesson. Each team is going to work secretly together. Your mission must be secret. What your group has to do is to 'make' the gesture in the book, and the other group has to guess it.

S3: Sounds fun. **You have to act in front of the other team?**[3]

T: That's right! You have 10 minutes! Take charge!!

S: Take charge!

Expressions used

1) **You mean you watched it yesterday night?** : The teacher is correcting the student's faulty grammar.
   선생님이 학생의 잘못된 문법을 고쳐주고 있다.

2) **They could be suffering from jet lag** : The teacher is making a joke about why the team lost. He is saying that they are tired because of the long flight and the jet-lag caused by the time zone differences. 선생님이 그 팀이 왜 졌는가에 대해 농담을 하고 있다. 그는 긴 비행과 시간 차에 의한 시차증 때문에 피곤하다고 말한다.

3) **You have to act in front of the other team?** : The student is asking the teacher if the 'gestures' activity must be done in front of the other teams of students.
   선생님에게 몸짓 활동을 다른 팀 앞에서 해야 하는가를 묻고 있다.

Scrabble

낱말 만들기

 철자를 결합하여 어휘를 만드는 게임에 대한 대화이다. 바둑판 모양의 네모난 칸에 각자가 가진 패(tile)를 놓아 어휘를 만드는 게임이다.

T: Good morning, ladies and gentlemen!

Ss: Good morning!

T: Today we are going to play a game. (After a few seconds of silence). Yah!!

Ss: Yah!!

T: The winners will get to take these delicious looking chocolate cakes!

Ss: Oh yeah!!

T: Let's split into groups of two

Ss: OK. (Move around finding partners)

T: Has anybody played Scrabble before?

Ss: No.

T: Here are the rules! This is the board, and these little squares are called tiles. There are numbers written on every tile. Those are the points that you get when you make a word out of them.

S1: If you think that is not word?

T: Not 'a' word you mean?

S1: Yes. If you think that is not a word what can you do?

T: Good question! If another team puts a letter and you don't think it's a word, you may challenge it.

Ss: ….

T: OK. For example, if I put 'schmph' on the board, is this a word?

Ss: No.

T: So then, if you think that is not a word, then you can say, 'I challenge that word!'. I will look it up in the dictionary. If that word is not in the dictionary, then I lose 10 points!

Ss: Oh!!

T: On the other hand, if 'schmph!' is in the dictionary, the team who challenged the word will be lose 10 points.

Ss: Ah….

T: Also, there are special squares that say double or triple word scores.

Ss: ….

T: So guess what that will do to your points. They will boost your points, right?

Ss: Yes.

T: **There is a 2 minute time limit for each turn.** [1] And if you can't come up with a word, you may change one, two, three, or four letters. No more than 4 letters. Any questions?

Ss: No.

T: Alright! Let's go! Take charge!

Ss: Take charge! (They start playing.)

T: OK. We have three teams. From each team pick a tile. **If**

you get a letter that is closest to **A**, you get to go first. [2]
(They each pick a letter.) So, what did you get?

Team 1: T.

Team 2: A.

Team 3: E.

T: So··· you (pointing at a student in team 2) get to go first. Then you (pointing a student in team 3). And finally, you (pointing at a student team 1).

(After the game is finished)

T: OK. Time's up! (Mr. Kim is a T.A.) Mr. Kim, do we have a winner over there?

Mr. Kim: **Yep, team 3 won by 4 points!** [3] It was a close game.

T: Wow! Only by 4 points? Sounds like a very close game. Good job, team 3!

Team 3: (very proudly) Heh heh··· thank you.

Teams 1 + 2: (stares at team 3 miserably.)

T: So then, we have a winner! Come on out and receive your prize!

Team 3: Woo hoo! (Rest of the students look at their prize hungrily.) OK. OK, we share···

T: So, are you going to share it with all the other students?

Team 3: Yes.

Scrabble

낱말 만들기

T: Great! Let's here it for team 3!

(Everybody starts cheering and clapping for team 3 and starts plundering their treasure.)

T: OK. Starting from next week, we have the oral examination. Here are what I will be evaluating you with: grammar, pronunciation, fluency, delivery, accuracy, etc.

S1: Oh, OK.

T: Any more questions?

Ss: No.

T: OK. Let's end our class here. Have a nice day!

Ss: Bye.

Expressions used

1) **There is a 2 minute time limit for each turn**: This is one of the rules of the games. The students have only two minutes in which to make a word with the letters they have. 이것은 게임 규칙 중의 하나이다. 학생들은 단지 2분 안에 그들이 가진 문자로 단어를 만들어야 한다.

2) **you get to go first**: You are first. 너가 처음이다.

3) **Team 3 won by 4 points! It was a close game**: The winning team — Team 3 — won the game with only four points more than the 2nd place team. The game score was close. 이긴 팀, 3번 팀은 2번 팀보다 단지 4점 차로 게임을 이겼다. 게임 점수가 아주 비슷했다.

Part 8

A few years ago I met an old professor at the University of Notre Dame. Looking back on his long life of teaching he said, with a funny twinkle in his eyes, "I have always complained that my work was constantly interrupted until I slowly discovered that my interruptions were my work".
[Henri Nouwen(1932~1996)Dutch Writer]

몇 년 전에 나는 노틀담 대학에서 노 교수를 만났다. 그의 오랜 교육 경력을 되돌아 보면서 그는 묘한 눈길로 말했다. "나는 항상 내 업무가 방해를 받는다고 불평했지만, 나의 방애물들이 내가 해야 할 일이라는 것을 서서히 깨닫게 되었다."

Others
기타

학습내용 ────────
여기에는 노트 준비의 필요성,
지각생에 대한 훈계, 상담 및
지시를 위한 E-mail에 관련된
대화를 정리하였다.

Notebook

 수업 중 공책이 필요한 이유에 대한 선생님의 설명이다. 선생님이 각자 두꺼운 공책을 준비할 것을 지시하자, 이에 학생들이 항의하고 선생님은 필기의 중요성을 길게 설명하고 있다.

T: Everybody show me your notebook.

Ss: Here! (Showing all different ones)

T: From next class, I want you to have a thick and good note-book; you can get it from a stationary shop.

Ss: Why? We all have our notebook. It's waste of money.

S1: Give me a reason why we have to buy a new notebook.

T: **Give me one good reason why you don't need one!** [1] I can give 100 reasons why you should. You are third-year students. If you'd had a thick and good notebook from first year throughout the third, your notebook would be full of important notes. If you think English is important then get yourself organized, start to jot down important points. You are future officers and also adults. **I can't always chase you up and make you do things.** [2] Get in the habit of doing things yourself. And trust me, if you note at least a few points down per class, in 4 years of school, that notebook could be very valuable to you. Understood?

Ss: Yes!

T: Great. **We got the point.** [3] Let's get moving, shall we?

Notebook 공책

Expressions used

1) **Give me one good reason why you don't need one**: The teacher is challenging the students to give him/her a reason why having a notebook in English class and using is unnecessary.
선생님이 학생에게 영어 수업에 공책을 가지고 이용하는 것이 왜 필요없는가에 대하여 도로 반박하고 있다.

2) **I can't always chase you up and make you do things**: The teacher is saying that he can't always make the students do things to learn. Much of the learning is the students' responsibility. In other words, the teacher is not going to treat the students like children. The students should be responsible for their own learning.
선생님이 학생들에게 배워야 할 것을 항상시킬 수 없다. 많은 부분은 학생의 책임이다. 달리 말하면, 선생님은 학생들을 아이들처럼 다루지 않으며, 학생들은 자신의 학습에 대해 책임을 져야 하는 것이다.

3) **We got the point**: We understand. 알았습니다.

Lateness

 지각하는 학생에 대한 선생님의 지도 방법을 설명하는 두 가지 예문이
다. 전혀 상반되는 두 가지 훈육 방법으로 자세히 검토해 보면 학생 지
도 및 영어 표현법의 습득에 도움이 될 것으로 보인다. (Rogers(2002)의
'Classroom Behaviour'(교실에서의 행동)에서 발췌하고 알기 쉽게 정리하
였다. 원어민 선생님이 영국식 영어로 된 담화를 미국식 영어로 재정리
하고 해설하였다.

상황 :

여학생, 멜리사(Melissa)가 아침에 지각하여 수업 중에 교실로 들어
왔다. 그런데 그녀는 학교에서 허용되지 않는 길게 매달리는 귀고리
(earrings)를 끼고 있었다.

··

A. Vigilant control (강한 제제)

T: (In a sharp voice) Come here. Why are you late?

S: I'm just a few minutes late.

T: Why are you wearing those⋯ things?

S: What?

T: Those things—you know what I'm talking about—those
stupid earrings.

S: Mrs. Daniels [the tutor teacher] [1] didn't say anything.
  (Melissa's tone is sulky, indifferent—she averts her eyes. She senses
  —yet annoyingly "creates"—a challenge.)

T: Listen, **I don't care what Mrs. Daniels did or didn't do**—

get them off. [2] You know you're not supposed to wear them! (He's clearly getting rattled now. He believes it's an issue on which he has to not only exercise discipline—he has to win.)

S: Yeah,—**well how come other teachers don't hassle us about it, eh?** [3]

T: Who do you think you're talking to? Get them off now and sit down or you're on detention!

Tip Cyclone, Hurricane, and Typhoon
Cyclones are usually called hurricanes in Europe and America. In the Far East and the Pacific they are usually called typhoons. (사이클론은 유럽이나 미국에서 허리케인이라 부른다. 극동과 태평양에서는 대개 태풍이라 부른다.)

Expressions used

1) **the tutor teacher**: A teacher who gives special help to students who need it in particular subject areas.
   특정 과목에서 필요로 하는 학생들에게 특별한 도움을 주는 선생님

2) **get them off**: Means, 'take them off' (the earrings).
   (귀걸이)를 떼어라.

3) **how come other teachers don't hassle us about it, eh?**: How come other teachers don't bother the students about wearing long earrings? 'Hassle' means to bother.
   왜 다른 선생님은 학생들이 긴 귀걸이를 끼는 것을 개의치 않습니까? 'Hassle'은 '들볶다'는 의미이다.

B. Relaxed control (온건한 제제)

T: Welcome Melissa. **I notice you're late** [1]; please take a seat. (Later in the lesson, when the students are working, she calls Melissa aside quietly.)
Melissa—you were late last period and the one before that; we'll need to have a brief chat after class.

S: (She moans.) Why? I couldn't help it.

T: Well, perhaps you can explain to me after class—I won't keep you long. (She quickly changes the focus.) Nice earrings.

S: What?

T: Nice earrings···

S: (Melissa grins with ill-concealed suspicion) Yeah.

T: **What's the school rule about earrings, Melissa?** [2]

S: But Mrs. Daniels didn't say anything in tutor group about them.

T: Maybe she didn't. I can check that with her. What's the school rule about earrings?

S: Yeah—well··· we're not supposed to.

T: Alright Melissa, it's my job to remind you, you know what to do. (She smiles.) I'll come and see how your work is going later.

Lateness

지각

Expressions used

1) **I notice you're late** : A polite way of saying, 'You are late!'
   '늦었다'는 말의 부드러운 표현이다.

2) **What's the school rule about earrings, Melissa?** : The teacher, rather than aggressively confronting the student about her earrings, is using a subtler, less aggressive approach, indicating that the student already knows it is wrong to wear long earrings to school. 선생님은 공격적으로 그녀의 귀걸이에 대해 대처하기보다는 다소 교묘하게 덜 공격적인 방식으로, 학생이 이미 학교에서 긴 귀고리를 끼는 것이 잘못이다라는 것을 지적하고 있다.

E-mail

선생님이 수업 전에 이메일로 학습 과제를 학생들에게 전송하므로 항상 이메일을 확인하고 강의에 참석하라는 지시문이다. 특히 선생님에게 이 메일을 보낼 때에는 교반과 이름을 반드시 적을 것을 지시하고 있다.

T: I forgot to tell you last week. When you come to class, you can check the schedule. **It helps us organize the class.** [1] I do have a couple of announcements this week: When you're sending your E-mails, please make sure you're sending both your name and your class. Some of your names are very unique, like 50-cent and Iris, but I have a lot of Brians and a lot of Roberts, so please make sure you do that. This week you should have received two E-mails from me. One was optional, and one was mandatory. Everybody?

Ss: Yes.

S1: What does 'mandatory' mean?

T: Mandatory. It is mandatory when you have to do something even if you don't want to do it, and it's optional when it is your choice to do it or not. It is mandatory that you read the e-mail, but do not answer the E-mail. I told you that if you have some ideas you want to share, please share it with the class. Some of you study English really well and you might want to share it with the class. But, you don't have to. It's optional. **Did anybody get to read the optional E-mails?** [2]

S1: (One student raises hand.)

E-mail

T: Only Anna?

S2: I'm sorry.

T: It's OK. It's optional. Do you think it's useful, Anna?

Anna: But I think it's hard to understand to use the websites.

T: Okay, some of the websites could seem a little bit difficult to use sometimes. If you have any problems please ask me, because once you learn to use the websites, I think they will be very useful.

Tip E-mail vs Snail mail

An E-mail address is made of a group of letters, numbers and dots, with no spaces in between any of them such as roknavy@co.kr. E-mail users often call the ordinary postal system 'snail mail' because they think it is so slow. (이메일은 숫자와 문자와 점의 집합으로 구성되며 그 사이를 띄우지 않는다.: roknavy@co.kr. 이메일 사용자는 종종 일상적인 우편제도를 너무 느리다고 '달팽이 메일'이 라고 부른다.)

Expressions used

1) **It helps us organize the class**: The teacher is explaining that using E-mail will help the class stay organized.
   이메일을 사용하면 수업이 잘 짜일 것이라고 설명하고 있다.

2) **Did anybody get to read the optional E-mails?**: The teacher is asking if the students read the 'optional' E-mails.
   선생님이 학생들이 이메일을 읽었는지 묻고 있다.

참|고|문|헌

- Chaudron, Craig. Second Language Classrooms: Research on teaching and learning. Cambridge University Press, 1988.
- Defense Language Institute. American Language Course. 1967.
- Ellis, R. The Study of Second Language Acquisition. Oxford: Oxford University Press, 2008.
- Grisewood J. N. Morris, Ting Morris. Children's Illustrated Dictionary. Miles Kelly Publishing Ltd, 1999.
- Heather Crossley. Illustrated Junior Dictionary. Kingfisher: New York, 1997.
- Malamah-Thomas, A. Classroom Interaction. Oxford University Press, 1987.
- Nefeldt, V. Webster's New World Dictionary. Simon & Schuster, Inc, 1997.
- Richard, J. C. and Charles Lockhart. Reflecting Teaching in Second Language Classrooms. Cambridge University Press, 1996.

원어민 영어 수업에 대한 원어민의 해설과 분석
원어민 수업 자료 모음집
(Collection of Native Teachers' Classroom Activities)

The secret of success is the ability
to survive failure.

(Noel Coward (English Palywright: 1899~1973)

성공의 비결은 실패에도
살아남을 수 있는 능력이다.

원어민 영어 수업 따라하기
현장교실영어

초판 1쇄 발행일 2011년 9월 6일

지은이 황기동
해설 및 감수 Gregory Goguts
펴낸이 박영희
편집 이은혜·김미선
책임편집 김혜정
펴낸곳 도서출판 어문학사
     132-891 서울특별시 도봉구 쌍문동 525-13
     전화: 02-998-0094/편집부: 02-998-2267
     홈페이지: www.amhbook.com
     트위터: @with_amhbook
     블로그: 네이버 http://blog.naver.com/amhbook
           다음 http://blog.daum.net/amhbook
     e-mail: am@amhbook.com
     등록: 2004년 4월 6일 제7-276호.

ISBN 978-89-6184-248-8 93740
정가 18,000원

이 도서의 국립중앙도서관 출판시도서목록(CIP)은 e-CIP홈페이지(http://www.nl.go.kr/ecip)와
국가자료공동목록시스템(http://www.nl.go.kr/kolisnet)에서 이용하실 수 있습니다.
(CIP제어번호: CIP2011003403)

※잘못 만들어진 책은 교환해 드립니다.